The Art of Speaking

Millett Wood

The Art of Speaking

David & Charles : Newton Abbot

ISBN 0 7153 5125 7

Set in 11/13pt Cornell
and printed in Great Britain
by Bristol Typesetting Co Ltd
For David & Charles (Publishers) Limited
South Devon House Newton Abbot Devon

With no lack of chivalry, the masculine gender has been used throughout this book – save where there is a difference to be stressed. Women can be most able speakers, often gaining a flying start by being better equipped in quality of voice.

Acknowledgements

I am most grateful to the following for reading the whole manuscript or specialised parts of it.

Notes and the appendix on Churchill, Sir David Pitblado (Joint Principal Private Secretary to Sir Winston, 1951-5) : the three chapters on Delivery, Dorothy Dayus (until recently professor of speech and drama at the Guildhall School of Music and Drama); The Lord Somers – John Somers-Cocks (professor at the Royal College of Music); Dr Brian Cardell (Reader in Pathology, King's College Hospital) : the Microphone, John Lindsey (Head of the Broadcasting Department, Conservative Central Office) : Visual Aids, Dr Clifford Hawkins (Lecturer in Clinical Medicine, the University of Birmingham) : Debate, Jasper Ridley (barrister and writer); Open-Air Meetings, Ivan Lawrence (barrister) : Television, Geoffrey Johnson Smith, MP; John Lindsey; James Wykes (Director of Educational Television, The Inner London Educational Authority).

The whole manuscript, James Margach (Political Correspondent of the *Sunday Times*); Dorothy Dayus; Denys Brook-Hart; Edward Brian; Michael Levete.

Contents

Preface

The almost universal attitude to speaking in public, to speaking on the feet, is an excellent example of the beloved habit of muddling through.

This book has been written for all, from all walks of life, from the youngest to the eldest, for man and woman : but at the present stage of the world's history it is directed particularly at the senior members of management – which includes chairmen and their boards – and at the professions. Mastery of this subject could be of such value that an appendix, entitled 'The Problem', examines the negative attitude towards it in industry and commerce, and in those professions becoming more and more entwined in business and public life. The appendix goes on to consider the basic question – at what age should it ideally be taught.

English is now the economic and, increasingly, the scientific language of the world. The legacy of this language, left by Britain to the present wide-ranging British Commonwealth, and the increasing enlargement of America's influence in the world, imply that crisp lucid speaking of well marshalled facts in English is a trump card to hold in the future – economically, politically and socially.

The title is chosen because the subject, even in its most practical application, is so much broader than speaking in public, and also on analogy with Quiller-Couch's lectures at Cambridge University a half-century ago on 'The Art of Writing' and 'The Art of Reading'.

Part 1

1 The Background and the Four Elements of Public Speaking

The key to speaking in public is the realisation that you are disclosing your personality. A man faces the fact that he cannot hide his foibles, his sensitivity and his emotions from his wife and close members of his family; but he does not like to put these at risk with strangers and, worse still, with colleagues and employees who know his standing in his business or profession. Apart from artists, from the painter to the international player of games, expressing themselves mainly in their skills, a man discloses his personality as much when he addresses an audience as at any time.

The tragedy is that nobody has explained to him why he is nervous. Nervousness, nervous tension, is simply Nature kindly warning him that he has a challenge to meet, be it mainly physical or mainly moral. (There are changes in the bloodstream and the muscles tighten up.) There is therefore no shame in such nervous tension; the shame, or cowardice, lies in refusing to face up to the challenge that it heralds.

Nervous tension, in a reasonable degree, is in fact an essential asset. No sprinter waiting to put on his spikes; no boxer waiting to put on his gloves; no actor waiting in the wings of a theatre; no musician awaiting his performance can possibly give of his best unless he has 'butterflies in the tummy', 'the needle'. It is the same for the speaker. But here the challenge is more subtle, for his personality remains at stake. The sprinter's tension ends as the pistol cracks; the boxer's normally as the first bell sounds; the actor has learnt his part and loses his personality in it; the musician, if need be, has the score before him. In contrast, the challenge to the speaker can continue throughout his effort as his voice frames his phrases and words to clothe his facts and thoughts. Let it be clear that any speaker who has not this sensitivity is handicapped; for he will lack the vital liaison with his audience by which he senses the speech is achieving its purpose.

How do you, therefore, harness this asset, which otherwise can destroy? Firstly, strive to gain such interest in the preparation of the speech, such intense happy preoccupation with the subject, that you lose yourself in the work – and have no time for introspection. Secondly, retain a sense of humour. You can only give of your best, and the ability to stand back and see yourself as others do gives a sense of proportion. It is particularly salutary to realise that worrying deeply can amount to a form of conceit. If, for example, you are proposing the toast of the bride and bridegroom and find yourself thinking just of your responsibility and disliking the thought of the happy occasion, remember that you, compared with the bride, living the greatest day of her life, are of minute importance. Thirdly, have confidence in your language – the words and the phrases that almost without thought you will use. Fortunately it is right to keep language simple and sentences short. Lastly, have – or gain – confidence in your voice. To speak well is a virile attribute. It is by no means a monopoly of the educated.

If the facts are accepted that speaking in public reveals a man's personality – regardless of his liking to speak or not, regardless of his being tough or sensitive in character – and that nervous tension is natural and must be made an asset, still a third important principle remains. Whether a speech be at the Royal Albert Hall, with an audience of 5,000, or a simple local meeting of ten or twenty people, it is essentially an enlargement of a responsible but friendly conversation between two, one being predominantly the listener. ('Responsible' means 'serious' not 'solemn', a distinction a number of people fail to appreciate.)

Oratory, the art of making public speeches in a graphic fashion – public speeches, as it were, in their own right – petered out in the House of Commons with Winston Churchill and Aneurin Bevan, and at the Bar soon after Birkett and Hastings. Even in its golden age, the fifth century BC, and in its second heyday, the Middle Ages, it often fell into disrepute, its standing in the latter times also being affected by the invention of the printing press. Today the pace of living obviates it. More particularly, television has ensured that there is far too much speaking, often of a very poor standard, whilst the use of the microphone indiscriminately at so many meetings deadens the quality of speech. In result, we are fast going to the other extreme and losing the dignity and authority of good speaking. (It would be of great benefit if members of the Bar, of the Church and of Parliament could stop the rot and set standards resting on these two qualities.) Oratory or not, it is a help to remember in making the point that a speech is essentially an enlargement of responsible conversation, that the pronunciation – and, to a degree, the presentation – of the best public speakers for many years has hardly differed from that of their home circle.

Imagine that you are relaxing for a few days in a country inn and one afternoon you and a stranger are kept in by heavy rain. Encouraged by your interest – on behalf of your son, about to leave school – he is persuaded to talk about his profession. Having cleared his head for a few seconds, he describes simply and logically the study entailed, the practical training to follow, the experience and specialisation marking the profession, how it knits in with the pattern of business, how it balances security and challenge, its potential remuneration and its future. And as he speaks, what is he doing? Is he keeping deadly still, like Lot's wife; like a man bound hand and foot; is his face as wooden as a ventriloquist's doll? The contrary is so. Almost the whole time he is looking you in the eyes. He pauses after every important point, to make sure by the look in your eyes that you are following him. It will be particularly at this time that his expression will be friendly.

He does not throw himself all over the place like a 'hot-gospeller' or an open-air orator. But his body, even although he is seated, is gently moving as he makes his points, ticking over like the engine of a car before it is driven away. He gestures from time to time. More particularly, his face takes up the look in his eyes, or, by a slight thrust of the chin or a lift of an eyebrow, emphasises the change of tone in his voice. The change of expression in his eyes and on his face will be in keeping with what he is saying.

Every one of these characteristics should be taken into public speaking, disciplined down or enlarged in keeping with the occasion. They embody the good manners to which every audience is entitled. More particularly, for the speaker they make speaking very much easier. Surplus nervous energy is given a healthy outlet and, more important still, unselfconscious movement of feature, of body or of forearms beats out the modulation of the voice and allows correct breathing. The speaker is being *natural*.

When potential pupils are being interviewed and are explaining their difficulties, their unaccountable nervousness, they are surprised when told they should speak in public rather like they are now doing. For they show their feelings in their expressions, in shrugging their shoulders slightly and gesturing simply as they smile.

From this conclusion another point follows. A speaker who, as he arises, noticeably alters his natural manner – in bearing, in expression and in voice – is an also-ran. Quite a number of politicians, when addressing their constituents, are in this class.

If this third principle is accepted, then clearly speaking in public is not an art to be isolated on a pinnacle. It is but the most important manifestation of speaking in general. Its principles apply to responsible talk throughout the day. They are almost as important in board meetings and in committees of all types, where there is the need both to inform and persuade, and also the need to speak lucidly after prepared thought yet to be able instantly, with no preparation, to cross swords skilfully. They stand in their own right in business negotiations and in dealings with important individual customers – by no means least in the export trade. They have equal weight for the professional man interviewing his clients. Again, layer after layer of the large organisations, at least, are in charge of many who have but a remote idea how to give instruction or advice clearly to those in their charge – with the result that time is wasted right down the line and much goodwill, and even morale, tragically lost. Such principles give lucidity of thought even before the mouth is opened. In every circumstance they save time, the god today of the rushing tycoon and his more relaxed colleagues. In other words, good natural speaking is a way of life. It is indeed a general discipline of unrivalled importance that can transform an individual, and so an organisation. There is a technique – in the original unmangled sense of the word – in the learning of all things, and during such training the process may appear artificial. But once the training to become a speaker is accomplished, then the resulting skill should be almost as much part of the man as his nervous and arterial systems.

These three principles – that when speaking in public you are disclosing your personality; that nervousness is natural, and is an asset to be harnessed; that *any* speech is but an enlargement of a responsible conversation with another – should always be in the back of your mind throughout the reading of this book. Their importance is fundamental.

Against this background, what are the elements of effective speaking? They are four. Firstly, there are the facts chosen and the thoughts of the speaker arising from them. These are the essence of a speech, without which it really cannot exist. With no reasonable content, it is so much candy floss.

Secondly, there is the language. Language should be simple and sentences short – language that the ordinary man and woman can understand. This does not mean, however, baby language and abrupt sentences. Moreover, an element of graphic language must be added – provided it is done naturally.

Thirdly, there is delivery. Certainly we speak with the voice; but the eyes and the expression of the face, the poise of the body and reasonable gestures of the hands and arms are inextricably linked with it.

It may help to compare these three elements with the human body. The facts and thoughts are the muscles and the internal organs which are all attached to the skeleton. If we tear a muscle or pull a tendon, if we rupture an organ, we limp about awkwardly. Similarly will a speech appear, if facts and ideas are disconnected and not logically arranged in a framework. As to the language and the delivery, these are akin to the clothes which are worn to keep the body warm; and which show also, in varying degrees, the character of the wearer.

Lastly, there is personality which, like our fingerprints, is unique to everybody. It would be exaggerating to *define* public speaking as the release of a man's personality; but it could well be *described* as such. Even if, as is so often the case, through nervous tension or shyness we conceal some of our qualities – such as sincerity, friendliness and authority – this remains true. Even if we go one stage further and try to conceal these weaknesses of nervous tension and shyness themselves by appearing 'tough', this remains true. If several persons, equally intelligent and equally knowledgeable about a subject are asked to speak about it to similar audiences, each speech would be different. Each would have some distinct facts and thoughts; and those facts and thoughts common to all would be differently arranged and differently stressed. Each speaker would have his own style in words and in sentence structure; each would have a different voice and manner.

2 The Preparation and Structure of a Speech

The object of any speech is to bring an idea – or a group of related ideas – and an audience together. This is achieved mainly by a logical appeal to their minds, but, at the right time, also by influencing their feelings.

Before preparing a speech, you should ask yourself three questions. Firstly, what is my particular object? Is it merely to inform or also to persuade? Is it to help, to advise or just to interest? Strictly, to inform must underpin every speech.

Linked with this question is the second – who is my audience? What is their knowledge of the subject? Are they experts, or intelligent without being experienced; of average intelligence or mixed intelligence? What is their age group? How large will they be – for size can affect an audience's attention and reaction? What will be their mood? Put yourself in their place not only before you start the speech but earlier, during its preparation.

Thirdly, how much time have I to speak? Even international chess and test cricket in England are governed by time. From the beginning, make Time your ally. If you are asked to speak for twenty minutes, make the speech run for eighteen to nineteen. The feeling of having time in hand can give the necessary relaxation to complement the nervous energy necessary to speak well. When you eventually come to deliver the speech, acquire the habit of laying your watch on the table just before you start. Even if the place be studded with clocks, this is a salutary discipline, and creates a good impression with the audience, who, whether you like it or not, are already eyeing you, beginning to size you up.

('What is my object?' – that paramount military principle turned into a question – surely has an application of great importance, broader than to this subject? How much time would be saved in administration, how many arguments in committee cut down to size if this simple phrase was imprinted on the minds of senior management and of the professions?)

The important things in life often require the simplest explanation. Nothing in this subject is more important than the preparation of a speech and to it this principle applies. Each with experience may evolve his own method, but the following sequence of three stages seems unrivalled.

Firstly, reflect on the subject. Circumstances will dictate how long before the speech you give the matter thought – the depth of your knowledge, the importance of the occasion, the length of the speech. A speech of thirty minutes might move you into action three to four weeks ahead. Sit down quietly for, say, half an hour with pen and large paper – the barrister's scribbling pad, of lined or unlined foolscap, is ideal – and write down higgledy-piggledy, all you know. Write legibly, none the less, for it makes rearrangement later so much easier. During the next seven to ten days, whenever your mind rests from work – when you are walking, driving, travelling in train or bus – turn the matter over in the mind. Slip a couple of postcards into the breast pocket – and down at once goes any new idea. It is extraordinary how flashes of insight strike you; how you become aware of relevant matter in the newspapers. Ask friends at lunch, at the club – forgoing your shyness – what they know of the subject; similarly, the family may contribute. Soon your random notes become quite a body. If from the beginning you have approached the speech as a challenge, interest begins to quicken.

Secondly, you must consider the structure of the speech, how you will arrange your facts and thoughts under headings. Without order, you cannot get properly into or out of a subject. It may be you will have to move, for a short disciplined while, into the third and last stage of preparation to gain inspiration; but ideally now is the time to erect the frame-work.

Lastly comes research, to fill in the details and give sinew to the speech. Such a task is not strange to many professions and business executives for reasons quite unconnected with speaking. This means a spell in the local reference library, the company's or club's library to consult your leading national journals, such as *The Times,* the *Economist* and the *Listener* for the last six or twelve months. The index for the first will be essential; skimming through the titles of the leading articles, possibly glancing at the headings of the correspondence, may be an alternative for the weeklies. (No index can be up-to-date; *The Times'* library is most courteous in helping to cover the gap, if you frame your request clearly.)

Again, for permanent reference, for any subject likely to come within the scope of a trained business, professional or academic mind, certain publications help to lay the foundation of confidence. Thus, in Britain, *Whitaker's Almanack;* the Stationery Office's *Britain. An Official Handbook* (reprinted around each February); the *Oxford Economic Atlas of the World;* indirectly, the *Economist* Diary, with its invaluable tables and statistics of matters at home and abroad – should all be on your desk. For more flexible use, although not a reference book proper, Anthony Sampson's *Anatomy of Britain Today* is admirable (all the more because it is written in a pungent style, often akin to that of a good speaker). Reference books of this calibre should be acquired in the various countries of the Commonwealth and in the United States.

Relevant pages of the papers and weeklies consulted will have to be 'flagged' with slips of paper; then the facts eventually selected noted up under the headings chosen by you in stage two of the preparation – joining those original facts and thoughts noted down in stage one. Always think with vigour as you research. To read is just to gather information; to think also is to develop power as well. As the facts you reflect on become increasingly part of you, so your own thoughts and conclusions start to grow.

Why is this threefold approach – reflection, deciding on the structure, and research – so strongly recommended? Because the essential feature of any good speech is 'Individuality'. If you research first, this vital quality is almost certain to be smothered in a wealth of impersonal and 'parrot-like' detail.

During the research, more and more keep in mind as you progress the factor of time – how long is the speech to be? For this must influence considerably the final selection of facts and thoughts. If you reluctantly conclude some valuable material must be cast, it may still be raised in question time. With no 'rigging', you might ask the chairman or your friends, if opportunity offers, to put the necessary questions.

If a speaker likes to make such preparation an onerous task, there can be no guarantee his speech will be effective. But given the challenge that greets anything worthwhile in life, this carving into shape of a speech can become absorbing – half the battle of making a good speech is already won; intense preoccupation with the subject leaves little time for negative introspection.

How does the chairman or managing director of a leading national company react to this preparation? If he has a speech of high importance, he will do well to prepare it himself. Churchill did. With experience, the task takes less and less time. Only if he has a personal assistant, or similar executive, of high calibre who knows his approach to affairs and his personal thoughts intimately, should he have the research and the outline done for him. It is advantageous if such executive is himself a speaker of experience. Discussion is then essential to fit the speech to his personality (discussion prior to the research would also be highly advantageous). Even so, such delegation remains of dubious value unless the speaker is highly experienced.

To have the preparation of a speech undertaken by a stranger, or even by anyone not knowing you intimately – particularly, as is sometimes the case, if there is no consultation – shows a cynicism and an insensitivity that deserves to prostitute the speaker's personality. The wound to the audience remains.

The final framing of a speech – the notes to be used when speaking – is so important that it takes up the whole of the next chapter. But how do you record the initial personal notes and those selected during research? Each to his own choice, but two or three sheets of plain foolscap for each of the headings selected during stage two of the preparation give you a sense of broadness, of room to manoeuvre. (Barristers' scribbling pads – books of foolscap – can have perforated sheets.) When you have recorded all you wish under the respective headings, first look through these notes and delete those that no longer appear of particular value. More especially bear in mind the time allotted for the speech; you may have to be quite ruthless in pruning it. Then comes the task of arranging the chosen facts, thoughts and argument under sub-headings. A reasonably wide margin will allow you to mark each point with the number or letter representing its allotted sub-heading and then its order under that sub-heading.

There are a number of principles underlying the final structure of any speech. Like a play, a speech must have unity. Four to five main headings are usually sufficient for any occasion. If there are too many the audience loses the thread of the story or the arguments (and so may the speaker). Headings should come readily to mind, but if in difficulty remember the chronological approach; the broader division into the past, the present and the future; the pros and cons of an argument; the division into contrast, and the cause and effect of a situation.

A good introduction is most important – as important as a smooth start to the sprinter. Already the audience are summing you up. You must remove the blanket between them and you as smoothly and as speedily as possible. Remember that the speaker and the audience are each part of a whole; rhythms of sympathy and antagonism can pass between them. If you do make a shaky start, then, like the sprinter who has faltered, you must determinedly try and make it up; but it is such an unnecessary handicap. The introduction should take up about a tenth of the speech. It should be related to the type of meeting and the type of audience. Normally, it will be partly of a general and partly of a particular nature.

In general, you might mention a personal connection – for example, that many years ago you were at school in this city; or, that your parents were born here. Again, show how aware you are of a matter of local interest – for instance the fame of the town's football club; that the village has won the prize for the best kept village in the county. Do not linger over such facts; just make a simple mention of them. Such an approach makes the audience begin to feel that you are one of them, and it introduces friendliness which, unabused, is a cardinal principle of speaking.

Humour, in its own right, is a tricky ingredient to use in the beginning. It is wiser never to attempt it in a part of the country whose sense of humour is not known to you. General friendliness is far the better.

A quotation, if apt and short (and spoken well) is a possibility. Like humour, it is best left to the experienced speaker, gifted with a relaxed naturalness.

Surprise, if really good, can be most effective, but it falls in the same category of experience as the use of humour or of the quotation. It requires too to be well spoken – to achieve the change in tone and pace that normally would be necessary.

As to the particular, leading in from a remark made by the chairman can be very effective. This can be done by arrangement, if need be, as the chairman is chatting with you before the meeting (the initiative would normally be his, to ask you whether he can help in his opening remarks). Done on your own initiative, it implies alertness and calmness. To outline the subject, if done crisply, is as good an approach as any, particularly if action from the speech is hoped for. Important as a good introduction is, do not linger over it. Drive into the heart of the subject as soon as possible – and as smoothly as possible.

A good conclusion is as important as a good introduction. The speaker must run right through the tape and not ease up a few feet before it. The test of a speaker is the impression of him that an audience takes away, and without being cynical, the end of the speech is their last of many impressions. It can be a crisp summary of what you have said; a call for action, or a quotation (if apt and short). Very important too is to show by the tone of your voice and by your bearing that you are concluding. No old fashioned peroration is necessary, but a note of pleasant authority should accompany the final words. It is essential to get smoothly into and out of a speech.

As a general rule, do not thank a chairman at the beginning of a speech, and never thank an audience at the end – in words. Good manners will indicate the exception when you do take up the chairman in a few words of acknowledgement. But to start with the theme song, 'Thank you, Mr Chairman', indicates nervous self-preservation, false bonhomie or oiliness. When the clapping fades after you have been introduced – and whilst the chairman is sitting down, you will have smoothly risen to your feet – pause around three seconds for the 'movement' of the audience to die down, then turn slightly towards the chairman and acknowledge his words by a relaxed bow from the shoulders – naturally, looking friendly. Then swing into the audience, hitting them at the back on the left with 'Mr Chairman', and, after a distinct pause, hitting them at the back on the right with 'Ladies and Gentlemen'. If you cut this down to a two-piece movement, acknowledging the chairman as you bow, these first two words will be muffled from the audience (whilst, when you are using a standing microphone, they will probably be inaudible as falling without the limited arc of traverse). When you end the speech – as just suggested, in a more authoritative tone and bearing – before sitting down, pause a second or so and bow similarly to the audience (perhaps a little more deeply).

Never apologise for lack of ability or lack of preparation. It is self-sympathetic or worse. Speaking is a deed, and those engaged in any form of action get on with it. You can be modest without being apologetic.

Just as colour can be given to language without its losing its basic simple meaning so colour can be given to the structure of a speech. This is achieved by the use of questions, and by the repetition of a phrase or a word. In rugby, if the 'scissors' movement in passing the ball is overdone, its sole object of creating surprise is defeated. In the same way questions must be judiciously used. They should be simple and correspondingly short; be spoken with the ring of query in the voice; and be followed by an effective pause. In a more disciplined way, they are particularly effective in outlining a subject in the introduction. The audience, still fairly sensitive as they continue to size you up, are alerted, fearing for the moment that they are going to be involved. But you have achieved your object – the pegs on which the speech will hang are well driven into their minds and they will await each in turn with unusual anticipation. (For example – 'Mr Chairman, Ladies and Gentlemen, ... I propose to deal with this subject by asking four questions . . . . The first, ... "What is the effect of X's action on Great Britain?" . . . . The second, ... "What is the effect of X's action on the European Economic Community?" . . . . The third, ... "What is the effect of X's action on the United States of America?" . . . . The fourth, ... "What is the effect of X's action on Russia?" . . . .') The ring of authoritative query and good pausing before and after each question are essential.

As the argument develops, repetition of a short phrase or a word at the beginning of chosen consecutive sentences can drive a point further into the listeners' minds. It can, as in the preceding paragraph, be linked with the question. It must never become ranting. Three to four times will suffice. In another sense, repetition of a complete thought expressed in different words or style may be necessary to fit different minds in the audience.

Humour is a pleasant ingredient in a speech, but there must be no strain about its introduction. It must be bent to the speech, not the speech bent to the humour. Friendliness of eye and of voice and the neatly turned phrase are better investments – even in after-dinner speaking. More speakers fail in trying to be funny than in any other way. Laughter is by no means the leading indication that a speech is being successful. Humour is best left to the experienced speaker, who is gifted in this way.

As to laughter, remember that when you do cause it to wait quietly and pleasantly; do not talk through it. Never laugh at your own jokes – unless you have 'dropped a clanger' and the joke is against yourself. Be sure, particularly if you are a politician, that your wife, when she is present at your speeches, is similarly disciplined.

The importance of keeping to time has already been mentioned. To carry on longer than arranged can often undo much of the good that you have achieved, and if you ever make this mistake, you should sense the audience losing interest. If you do find that you need more time – and are satisfied that the audience is still interested – turn to the chairman for sanction. Probably he will seek the meeting's agreement and, in such a way, goodwill is maintained. A chairman may have to ask a speaker to conclude his speech if the latter does not take such an initiative. This can be a depressing experience. Particularly if you are speaking in a lunch hour – many learned societies have such meetings – remember the time of many present must be limited. If you are one of a panel of speakers, the discipline of time is absolute. Disobey it, and a good speech, most carefully prepared but for this omission, can be throttled.

This making of Time your ally implies a rehearsal. The best method is to lean your notes on a mantelpiece above which there is a mirror. Place near the notes your watch, a spare card and a pencil. Rehearse the speech in approximately sessions of five minutes, stopping where a natural break occurs. Note the time on the spare card and move away for a minute's relaxation. Follow such a sequence until the speech is finished.

Such a method ensures that you keep to the general pace you have selected in the beginning for your task, neither getting faster and faster, nor, more rarely, becoming sluggish. The mirror is not so much to look in as to give you the company of a moving shape as you traverse the imaginary audience. Use your imagination, and believe that the audience is present; and, although not in power, essentially in pace and pausing link up with it.

Until you become an experienced speaker, do not complicate this simple process by using a tape recorder. Tape recorders are not essential to help potential speakers. If you wish to use one, settle the time element first, as just described, and use the recorder in a second rehearsal. The danger to avoid, at all costs, is becoming too elaborate in preparation, so that much essential spontaneity is lost and the event becomes wrapped in too much importance – conceit starts to thrust its head in. As in athletics and games, over-preparation can be as bad as under-preparation.

If you are speaking so much that time really does press, then experience will let you gauge the overall length of the speech by rehearsing only part (just as a writer estimates the length of his script by checking a few pages). Check yourself to be *within* the time allowed – a minute or so – in order to feel relaxed, not having to speak against the clock. Remember that although you are adopting this procedure to conform to the time allotted to you, what you are doing should still be regarded as a full-blooded rehearsal – making sure that the delivery is satisfactory, that the facts and ideas link in smoothly and that you are neither being verbose, nor long in your sentences.

Much good may come from talking over the speech with an alert and wise friend, or a sympathetic but candid member of the family. Such a conversation may be a tonic, showing up the facts and ideas, leading to their modification or replacement and, perhaps, altering the emphasis of what you have to say. You can get so close to the subject that you cannot see the wood for the trees. If you have a rehearsal with such a friend present – now judging not only the subject matter but the whole production – remember his reaction, unless he himself is an experienced speaker, may be more favourable than that of an audience made up of strangers. Apart from the fact the challenge for you is not the same, he, *knowing* your personality, may assume you are revealing it as a matter of course, whereas many good people conceal much of their character when speaking in public.

3 Notes

Keep your notes as simple as possible. Once you are on your feet, you, the audience and the notes should be in balance. Too elaborate a note and you cannot properly hold the attention of the audience. Too scanty a note and you may begin to wander or waffle.

For notes, cards are unrivalled. Postcards, or rather the thinner 'record' cards supplied by commercial stationers, are the ideal. Their essential characteristic is that they lean, without which, unless held, no notes can be easily consulted (for rarely is a desk lectern made at steep enough angle). One card or several make no difference, they are so compact. Number them, and they interchange easily, and if you drop them the catastrophe is not that which occurs with paper notes. They do not obtrude on the meeting. They keep, if need be, for months.

If you propose to hold the cards, cut them in half, so that they nestle in the palm of the hand. Holding them in the finger tips recalls a choir-boy – and the other hand inclines to slip up in sympathy. Half cards are particularly suitable for after-dinner speaking or in any situation – such as summing up a tour 'en route' for visitors to a factory – where you are standing unshielded by table or platform.

Whether you propose to hold or to lean the cards, write your notes so that the height of the card is greater than its width. This is essential for holding, advisable in both cases so that you do not waste writing space.

What should be so obvious must be stressed – a speech must not be read. It is the surest way to conceal your personality. Naturalness, friendliness and authority are largely, if not completely, lost, and consequently no sympathetic impulse is created in the audience's mind. You cannot, as you should, look at them almost the whole time that you are actually speaking. Again, the language of writing and of speaking are different. Even if you write in 'speaking' language, the attempt to use a speaker's voice when able to look up so much less will have very limited success. The upshot is that you are unintentionally being ill-mannered. (If the word 'personality' has too strident a sound for you in this age of jargon and false values, and you decide that not to reveal your personality is becoming, offset this false modesty and give of your natural best by speaking for the sake of your organisation or of the cause that you are supporting and, always, for the sake of the audience.)

All day each of us speaks spontaneously, hardly ever thinking about the words we use but just of the facts and ideas in our heads. No managing director, no foreman or housewife dreams of pulling out a written document from which each respectively speaks to his secretary, to the men in his control or to her family.

It is not without wisdom that the rules of procedure governing the two Houses of Parliament forbid the reading of speeches, except when Ministers and leaders of the Opposition are making considered statements of policy at the despatch box – a concession to the pressure of modern government. (It is true that some members of the Commons who are not particularly competent on their feet use quite detailed notes and are often generously treated by their colleagues; but if they fail to look up within reason, or circumstances of business press, they are quickly called to order. The House of Lords, in keeping with its more relaxed character, inclines to ease the rule slightly more.) Many societies throughout the land in their rules follow Parliament's strict precedent in barring such reading.

Why, then, are tens of thousands of meetings yearly put in purgatory by this practice of over-insurance against risk; a practice that sucks out all the red corpuscles from the body of

c

a contribution? There are a number of reasons, positive and negative. Positively it is for three, mentioned in the background to speaking in chapter 1 : – that those addressing audiences so rarely understand that a speech is inevitably linked with their personality; that nervousness is a friendly warning by Nature of a challenge, not to be sidestepped but to be met and conquered; and that speaking in public is just the disciplined enlargement of a responsible conversation between two, one of whom is predominantly speaking. Consequently, they refuse to let go of the side of the bath and strike out and swim. Unbroken fluency is far from essential. Occasional hesitation in speech is natural and is appreciated as such by those listening; whereas to voice words not chosen in their presence has a cold vacuum-like effect which they are apt to resent.

If the very worst happens and you do dry up – not in the least inevitable, nor in the least usual – you are not in everlasting disgrace. Disraeli's first speech in the House of Commons was far from a success. The story of the pedigree bull terrier walking down the village street with his master illustrates the point. One morning, he was bowled over and mauled by the butcher's mongrel. The next day, the mongrel rushed out of the shop again. In a minute he was fighting for his life. In another minute, he had lost it. Therefore, if you do dry up, seize the first opportunity to come back and speak, and show what you are made of. Such experience, although not to be sought for, might purge you of trouble for all time.

Negatively, a number of causes encourage this lame habit. This is indeed an age of pressure, and lack of time for preparation can rightly be occasionally claimed by the best of us as speed becomes rush when outside influences take charge. Secondly, conveners of conferences aggravate the position by their unimaginative custom of demanding a copy of a script weeks, if not months, ahead of the occasion so it can be reproduced in a record of the conference or in a trade journal. All would be well if they gave up the snobbery of using the term 'reading a paper', and made it quite clear to the speaker that they wished him really to speak, and not drone through a copy of his script. Again, linked with the last point, at all varieties of meetings there is a tendency to hand out copies of a speech to the press whenever they are present, until they have come to regard possession as of right. If it is a question of a formal statement of responsible action, for example, by the president of a national body where it is wished to make the statement crystal clear; or, if it is a question relating to finance and so governed by Stock Exchange hours; then a handout is in its own right. But other than at press conferences proper, this habit seems to be a matter of prestige for the holders of business assemblies, or a fear that the press will produce a mutilated account of a speech unless doubly briefed. Accordingly, except when the speaker is properly advised, as suggested above – or is experienced and master of himself – he tends to stick slavishly to the written text and becomes just an impersonal announcer, so defeating the object of the conference of instructing and interesting those present. Organisers of meetings should realise, like the clergyman, that they cannot please everybody, and it is best to give priorities their place.

If you are worth your salt, whenever you may be asked to forward an advanced draft of your contribution to a conference, do one of two things – other than protesting. Either prepare such draft and then, before despatching it, reduce it to notes for your speech; or, assemble, 'card' the notes for the speech and from them dictate to your secretary the draft. Without doubt the second method is superior. It gives priority where it is due, and the dictating provides a first rough rehearsal of the speech. It guarantees also that the language of the draft retains to a degree the personal touch of speaking to an audience. When the draft is typed, certainly you should polish it for its more permanent state

Then if the facts of modern life are too strong to be resisted and the Press request an advance copy – even as late as on arrival – the organisers of the conference, or yourself running your own meeting, can let each have a copy of such long-flowing draft. If need be, you can announce firmly but with friendliness as you begin the speech 'I assume the Press, who I understand have a long-flowing draft of this speech, will not expect me to be so discourteous to my audience as to read such draft. They have my assurance that what I say will follow entirely the sequence of it'.

Obviously there are occasions when circumstances permit no option to the reading of a draft – sudden pressure of work or, more particularly, a sudden request by an outside body. Even then, to do so well, a man must be already an experienced speaker. If everyone realised how much reading a speech belittled him – and his organisation or profession – in the eyes of his audience, he would give the same measure of attention to speaking in public as he gives to his responsible business transactions. Speaking should be as much a deed as any skilful performance in games, in sports and in the arts. It should not be an ordeal but an adventure. Too many adopt a negative or at least an apologetic approach. Industry and commerce and the professions must go over to the attack.

When *do* you read a paper? This is a term that should be reserved for the scientist, the technologist, the medical specialist and any specialist of merit who is dealing with a subject so intricate that a skeleton of notes is hardly possible. The notes would be almost as long as a draft, and their complicated structure more a distraction than a help to their author. Reading a paper is an art in itself. It entails looking at the audience whilst reading quite a quarter of the time, so as to keep their interest and retain your authority. It is essential, as in a speech, that you put yourself in their frame of mind, on their level of knowledge, in order that you can measure your pace and judge your length of pause correctly. If the paper is of the highest importance, do not write it out in normal sentence and paragraph, but let each sentence, or important thought stand out by itself (like the lines of the psalter, or the verse of a poem). You must hope that the organisers have had the acumen not to take away the freshness of your contribution by distributing copies before your address (it would be wiser to ensure this beforehand).

Memorising a speech is another apparently alternative form of insurance, but often more dangerous than reading it. While you can look towards the audience, you cannot properly look *at* them. For all the time you are mentally looking backward to remember your brief – the actual words rather than the thoughts and facts. The look in your eyes is apparent to an experienced observer; it is that of a sightless man. You cannot risk the distraction of catching the eye here and there of a member of the audience as you skim over them. Instead of being on the attack you are on the defence. The vital link with your listeners is broken; spontaneity and all naturalness are missing. Like reading, memorising comes neither from the mind nor the heart, and in consequence it is mechanical. It is a brittle tactic – if you are interrupted, accidentally or by deliberate questions; if you forget . . . Freemasons should be particularly careful to distinguish the custom of their elaborate ritual from the resilience required to deliver a speech.

Speaking demands a forward drive. The best example is the barrister arguing from a well annotated brief, and building up his case as events unfold. To be sure, the analogy is not quite fair, for the framework of most speeches is complete beforehand. But the challenge of finding the words and the phrases; realising the need of looking at those you are addressing; mirroring your facts and ideas in your features and bearing – is common to advocacy and speeches prepared in advance.

'Notes' is a word of different interpretation to different people. They are *your* notes to be stamped by *your* individuality. Yet there are some common principles invaluable to all speakers. Notes are a courtesy to the audience, not a crib for the speaker. Do not furtively conceal them low down under your coat front and there gingerly refer to them. How pleased an audience are, as they begin to run their eyes over a speaker, to see him lay down his watch and take out a few cards – the initial discipline of speaking is being revealed. Likewise resting cards flat on the table, at crutch level, is obviously wrong.

It can easily lead to leaning on the table – and so to 'duck's disease'. Not only is this ugly, but worse than the throat being creased as you look down, so spoiling the quality of the voice, is its being stretched as you try and look up, so also possibly straining the vocal cords.

The fact that you make the notes on cards should not hypnotise you into cramming as much on a card as if it were a stamped postcard. Spacing is nearly as important as legibility. As to legibility, it is such a tragedy when great care is taken over the preparation of a speech and it is then cast in writing so bad that, blended with bad spacing, it puts your whole bearing in hazard as you crane forward, losing poise of body and authority of feature. Notes should be clearly visible at a range of about three feet. Always hold or place the cards so that they are roughly in line with your eyes and the centre or the back of the audience – the latter, unless the numbers are large (say, 1,000 or more). This is an essential principle of good speaking – there is *no* alternative. If you decide to hold the cards, the hand and the forearm act as a mobile lectern bringing the cards *up and forwards* towards the eyes when you wish to refer to them. Meanwhile they can comfortably rest in the palm of the hand held across the body in the hollow of the ribs. Feel the upper arm just clear the ribs as you move the hand up and forwards. Alternatively, you must have some object on which to rest and lean the notes. Each will have his preference, although circumstances may dictate which is the better. A separate support gives the more freedom and allows of a full-sized card. The fact that by tradition such an aid is rarely provided gives a splendid opportunity to speakers to slough off their shyness and gently yet firmly demand it. There is no need for a formal lectern (rarely, in any case, adjustable to suit varying heights). Improvising, if done with quiet natural dignity, has its merits. Books or telephone directories will do. A neatly rolled overcoat, a couple of small lampshades borrowed from a wall bracket have been used. Then you *must* 'top' such support with a small article against which the cards can lean. Whether you smoke or not, a packet of 20 cigarettes slipped in your pocket provides one satisfactory answer.

Check that the light, natural or artificial, is satisfactory – standing up in your speaking position to do so. When you are to speak in artificial light, avoid making notes in pencil which can so easily shine (pencil, in all cases, should be only a make-shift).

Be sure, in sum, that you will be as comfortable as possible when you stand up to speak. The audience also will benefit from such care. For your part, ensure the notes are clearly legible and well spaced (perhaps varied in depth to bring out the varied importance of the sub-headings and, if need be, well indented). Underline, in reason, and if it really helps, use red or another coloured ink to make a point stand out (but do not turn the notes into a rainbow). If an important point would fall too near the bottom of a card, to avoid turning over leave the bottom blank and start the point on a fresh card. A margin of at least one inch will allow any additions or alterations that may be necessary if you are one of many speakers. Remember the basic simplicity of notes – some subjects may lend themselves to simple tabulation on one card. Do have the fibre to demand your 'lectern' and any other reasonable aid.

If you wear spectacles, think out the consequences; for you depend on the expression of the eyes greatly in speaking. Do avoid the frequent taking off and putting on of them that distracts the audience so easily from your speech. It may be that well-spaced writing or typing in large letters, which allows you to stand well back wearing no glasses at all, will be the solution. If you use bi-focal spectacles, be sure of the height of the notes being accurate, so that you are comfortable in stance and do not appear stiff-necked. For those requiring help only in reading, and mature or virile enough to wear them with aplomb, half-glasses are the solution. Make sure that your glasses are good in appearance; this should not be regarded as a luxury.

Without trespassing on each person's individuality, are there any guidelines as to the type of note suitable as the final product of preparing a speech? Imagine that your wife kicks over the traces one Saturday morning and that you are ordered to take over some formidable week-end shopping. What do you do? You write down, possibly on the back of an envelope, the shops and places to visit – the butcher, the baker, the grocer, the bank, the fruiterer, the confectioner and the post office. Then, if you are wise, you rearrange the order so that your calls are in easy sequence, and fill in the items to be dealt with at each. Better written and better spaced and on plain cards, but similar in structure, is your speech. Facts link into facts and thoughts into thoughts. Each heading has detail simply set out beneath it.

Again, you have a very important letter to write, too difficult to be dictated directly. You resent the idea of writing it out in longhand. Accordingly, you jot down ideas, rearrange them in correct order and dictate the letter from this final note. Well carded, your note would resemble those of a speech.

You wish to move house. You decide first of all to have a word with your friend, the family solicitor. If you are wise, before the visit you will sit down and assemble all the apparently relevant points – the maximum price that you are prepared to pay, the conditions in the chosen area of travel by road and rail, the shopping facilities and the likelihood of 'development' – trunk roads, airports, electric pylons, gasometers and suchlike. Again, you rearrange in sequence. When you and your wife call at his offices, you rest the notes on your crossed knees, ask his permission to lead in, and logically unwind the problem. The analogy to notes for a speech holds. Here is your pattern, whether addressing 5,000 at the Royal Albert Hall, probably with more detail filled in, or speaking to twenty people at a local meeting, the outline remaining simple.

If you are proposing to make an apt quotation – not an extract from a journal or a periodical – certainly write it out in full, *not* to read it but to refresh the memory before you speak it. Do this either on the back of the card, or, in different

NOTES 41

coloured ink near the relevant note. Mark up the notes where you propose to refer to an extract from an actual document or paper – which you will, in the proper tone, read.

Do remember that good facts and ideas are the sinews of a speech – its only justification. Therefore, avoid generalities. Avoid also gimmicks; they bite into and lessen a man's individuality and dignity, and so his authority. Likewise on all occasions avoid smut. Those who laugh at the time will not respect you more when the occasion has worn off and you will lose the respect of many right away. Never indulge in the nonsense of marking where you should make a gesture, for, as explained later, gestures are irrefutably co-ordinated with the voice, and must be spontaneous.

Winston Churchill is said to have read his speeches on most occasions. Lloyd George is said, in the main, to have memorised his. Such statements, without explanation, appear to undermine all the principles set out in a book such as this. When the facts are examined, they are bound to support them. In an appendix, the facts are fully investigated, and include sufficient description of Sir Winston's early life and the background of his times to explain how he came to his style of speaking. The beginning and the end at least of this appendix are highly relevant to any reader.

4 Language

Language is the second element in speaking. It should be simple, basically the vocabulary of ordinary people. Similarly, sentences should be short – not abrupt – so that neither the speaker nor the audience gets lost. It is a salutary lesson for a speaker to hear himself on tape and to notice the prolonged length of so many of his sentences. Language and sentences in speaking and language and sentences in writing are normally very different. There is more formality in the fully developed written sense.

Simplicity does not mean dullness. Language can still be graphic without losing simplicity. Subject to what is said later about the cliché, a certain 'colour' gives balance and adds interest. At school, we heard about figures of speech, notably the simile and the metaphor. The fact we may have forgotten these terms may be no matter of self-censure but may well mean, so used have we become to speaking them, that they are part of us. Illustrative language, based on analogy and contrast, often can replace effectively normal language not quite adequate for the occasion. The pictorial appeals to every type of person and often to all ages. Here are some simple examples.

'I was out on a limb.'
(I was in an awkward situation and did not know what to do.)
'Gentlemen, this argument is generating more heat than light.'
(Gentlemen, we seem to be letting our feelings overcome our sense of judgement.)
'That manager is always fighting against the collar.'
(That manager is always putting up difficulties, behaving obstinately.)

'We shall have to ride out the storm.'
(We shall have to wait until the crisis in the Country is over.)
'We must apply a touch of the brake.'
(We shall have to slow up a little [or, from time to time].)
'Who's going to foot the bill?'
(Who's going to take responsibility for this?)
'We shall have to throw in the towel.'
(We shall have to give up this project.)
'Roberts used to lay back his ears and make for the line.'
(Roberts used to run with great determination for the line.)

The metaphor as illustrated in short simplicity above is the ideal figure of speech. It can be more succinct than the simile. It implies one thing *is* another; the simile states one thing is *like* another. The simile in its simplicity represents the most natural of all things – comparison. It was the greatest weapon of Christ's teaching. Here are some simple examples of this figure of speech.

'England sensed their chance and made like tigers for the kill.'
'He ran like the wind.'
'As light as a fairy.'

As suggested, we use figures of speech daily without thought. What we want to do is to enlarge such use, but only in quality. There must never be any straining after effect. Figures of speech can be lengthened without losing their effect.

'Making speeches that would have made Mr Krushchev look like a member of the Primrose League.'
'The Conservative Party looked like an ants' nest that had just received a nasty dose of boiling water.'
'Britain's endeavour to enter the European Economic Community has been like a person trying to board a moving bus which did not know its destination.'
'. . . using the Jews as a lightning conductor for popular storms.'

Colour also comes by apt choice of words. Apart from their value in their own right – for beauty or for aptness – words may be a dilution, as it were, of the figure of speech. For example :

'The jack-booted arrogance of the local government official.'
'The modern twenty-storey skyscrapers, with their clinical air of efficiency.'

Quotations – poetical, historical and of modern thought – if apt, short and spoken well are very valuable. As with humour, their use must show no sign of strain, of distorting the content of the speech – 'apt' is a small but healthy word.

Slang, of a 'respectable' kind, is a blood brother to figures of speech.

Just as the asking of questions must not be overdone in seeking colour of structure, so graphic speech must be used judiciously. A speaker not well equipped in words must be careful not to become pretentious, thus putting at stake his naturalness. In contrast, one well equipped, and at the same time, an experienced speaker, must guard against his language being so attractive that, despite the high quality of his facts and reflections, the audience waits more on the quality of his words.

Many intellectually well equipped in their own work – for example, Harley Street specialists, highly qualified engineers – are perturbed because life of recent years has left them no time to read regularly, and so to keep reasonably fluent. Nothing can replace a love of language, not to the depth achieved by a scholar but to the extent that you rarely are at a loss for the right phrase. Yet a stop-gap remedy, pleasant and sensible if discriminately used, is to devote occasionally, for around a month, five to ten minutes daily to reading from a responsible newspaper – for the *language*. Read one of *The Times'* leaders or an article of one of their foreign correspondents, political correspondents, or sports writers.*

Note down any figures that appeal to you, and look through

* There is a disturbing tendency in *The Times* of late, particularly among the sports writers, to mix their metaphors. Steer clear of this. (e.g. 'David Hemery's dramatic spread-eagling of the hurdles field lit a fire under public interest and there are signs that it has not yet gone off the boil'. '. . . there was little Johnstone – as always as elusive and as annoying . . . as some wasp at a picnic – to worm his way brilliantly down the right, push a diagonal pass inwards for Murdoch coming up full steam to crash in goal number two.')

the list at the week-end. If, on reflection, they really fit your style, bear them in mind and gradually you will be using them yourself in conversation. Thus a habit can be acquired, enjoyable in itself, which could stimulate you to deeper study.

The trend to specialisation and the rush of life in this complicated age have introduced much speaking and much writing of jargon – unintelligible words, distorted word forms and debased language. Newspapers – to be sure, working under tremendous pressure of time and often restricted in space – have long been guilty. The advertising agencies in their conversation do their share of distortion. Not a few of the books written to educate management are crammed with jargon. Not a few prospectuses or actual timetables of management courses are in their language bad advocates for their sponsors' desire to enlarge and re-orientate the minds of the students.

A common example of jargon is the current passion for forming new nouns ending in '-tion'. 'Confrontation' was the 1966-7 favourite. General de Gaulle's 'participation' came across the Channel in 1968. The shipping lines introduced 'containerisation' in 1969 - whilst in the last month of that year, *The Times'* Educational Correspondent, of all people, talked of 'comprehensivisation'. To chisel down language to a reasonable perfection is always the object, but to compress it by such monstrosities is bad.

A recent circular from one of the bodies in Britain engaged in the education of management stated : 'For research purposes and to enable us to provide a national perspective on management course provision and utilisation we should be glad . . .' Why not open it out a little? 'To enable us to offer a national perspective on what provision is made for management courses and how much they are used, we shall be glad . . .' Jargon is equally to be avoided in speaking.

Avoid the cliché, and empty link phrases – 'I am sure you will agree' – 'Far be it from me . . .' – 'I think . . .' – 'Now' or 'Well now' and similar words. Read the late Sir Ernest Gowers' note on the cliché in his *ABC of Plain Words*. His simple treatment of the subject is unrivalled. A cliché, in the broad sweep, is any hackneyed phrase once of good application but since over-used or badly used. It covers metaphors such as 'leave no stone unturned', 'explore every avenue'; facetious or lengthy ways of saying simple things such as 'conspicuous by its absence'; and threadbare phrases such as 'leave severely alone', 'the acid test', 'the psychological moment'.

'Ers' and 'ums' are caused by not clearing the mind before speaking. This may be due to nervousness, having nothing to say or the habits of conversation. Remember that pausing is an essential part of the pattern of speaking.

Style for a speaker is a combination of the language he chooses and his delivery. Good speakers, within reason, vary their style to blend with their object and their audiences. The rhythm of speech depends largely on the phrasing chosen. Never strain after style for its own sake, for naturalness then goes.

English is the greatest of all languages – the most expressive and flexible. In brilliance of conversation, French alone can approach it. In public speaking and forensic skill in court, at their highest standing, it has no rival. In poetry of all types – lyrical, epic and dramatic—it stands alone.

There is no short cut to the mastery of any technique, and in the case of skill in the use of language, good reading as a habit is the basis. 'Reading maketh a full man' said Bacon; for the complement to fluency in speech is affluence in thought. It is true that if you let thought govern your language then style is apt to follow. But to begin with, a certain deliberate concentration on the phrasing used, as well as the thought expressed, is needed. In the course of time, this will not be necessary, for the substance and the form – the thoughts and the words chosen – are really one and indivisible.

A good dictionary (the latest edition of the *Concise Oxford* with its prefaces and notes on etymology and pronunciation is unsurpassed), Roget's *Thesaurus of English Words and Phrases* and Gowers' twin volumes, *Plain Words* and the *ABC of Plain Words* (now published as one by Her Majesty's Stationery Office) should be on every responsible person's

desk, at the office and at home. Roget should be available in
most English-speaking countries : Gowers should be acquired
by hook or crook. Look at these books as constant, happy companions, not as necessities bought out of discipline. Gowers
will repay reading right through as soon as possible.

A regular half-hour daily with a good quality newspaper is
a priority. The reading of great prose is an excellent habit.
The Authorised Version of the Bible – set out to be read as
literature – comprises many books of the greatest merit. But
the greatest aid of all is the reading, then speaking, of well
chosen poetry.

Poetry is the quintessence of language, expressing thoughts
with a wonderful economy of words – hence its outstanding
value for speakers. Here, at their best, the words are not the
mere dress of thought but the thought itself. Britain's greatest
contribution to the arts of the world has been its poetry. If
you have any doubts of its manly virtues, start by reading
Lord Wavell's collection *Other Men's Flowers* – with its racy
preface and notes. Men of action through the ages have
believed in its inspiration to give courage and vision and comfort of mind in trouble – Lord Allenby (Wavell's counter-
part in World War I) and Churchill amongst them.

Shakespeare must stand in his own right. His mastery of
words is almost equalled by his unrivalled knowledge of
human nature. George Rylands' collection, *The Ages of Man*,
dividing excerpts of Shakespeare into Youth, Manhood and
Age, is an excellent introduction to the sonnets and plays.

Broadening the issue – after all, good speaking affects the
complete personality of a man and woman – remember the
Caliph's remark to Hassan in Flecker's play of that name :
'If there should ever arise a nation whose people have forgotten
poetry . . . what of them?' Appreciation of good verse would
do much to loosen the tension of modern life; would help us to
sort out the things that matter from the dross increasingly
surrounding us. 'Where there is no vision, the people perish.'

Poetry in the main must be spoken – quite quietly if desired;
Lord Wavell is as good a mentor as any in this matter. The

merits of poetry are enlarged on in chapter 8, dealing with the voice. Poetry, when it is properly spoken, draws together the three elements of speaking common to us all – quality of thought, of language and of delivery (to be permeated by the fourth element, unique to each of us, our personality).

In conclusion, here are some verses from Tennyson's poem, 'The Brook'. In its complete thirteen verses are 309 words. Of these, 225 are of one syllable, 82 of two, 1 of three and 1 of four syllables.* Here is an outstanding example of the simplicity of language. Yet it is full of imagery and of sound; and the words chosen to describe the brook's progress bring it wonderfully alive.

> I come from haunts of coot and hern,
> I make a sudden sally,
> And sparkle out among the fern,
> To bicker down a valley.
> . . . . . .
> I chatter over stony ways,
> In little sharps and trebles,
> I bubble into eddying bays,
> I babble on the pebbles.
>
> With many a curve my banks I fret
> By many a field and fallow,
> And many a fairy foreland set
> With willow-weed and mallow.
> . . . . . .
> I slip, I slide, I gloom, I glance,
> Among my skimming swallows;
> I make the netted sunbeam dance
> Against my sandy shallows.
>
> I murmur under moon and stars
> In brambly wildernesses;
> I linger by my shingly bars;
> I loiter by my cresses;

---

* It is right to say that 'many', used five times, is treated as one syllable: and 'eddying' and 'silvery' (not shown) are treated as two – for the sake of scansion.

And out again I curve and flow
To join the brimming river,
For men may come and men may go,
But I go on for ever.

Ivor Brown, in his wise and magnificent book, *Shakespeare,* shows how Shakespeare used monosyllables with great effect when circumstances demanded (notably for pathos or to frighten). Longer words must have their place, but simplicity remains the key.

5 The Three Essential Qualities of a Speaker: Nervous Tension

All our powers of mind and body come to us in a state of imperfection. The purpose of all training – in games, athletics, ballet dancing, singing, speaking and countless other activities – is development, if not to perfection, at least to a reasonable standard of skill. Speaking is an art and, although, as has already been said, it cannot be defined as such, it can be described as the release of personality. This itself is a blend of mind and temperament. Moreover, each of us has several personalities, or shades of personality, and, ideally, the *whole* balanced individual should be shown when speaking – the blend of all our personalities.

Three qualities a speaker must possess – sincerity, friendliness and authority. Many speakers, without possessing the perfect balance of these three characteristics, make outwardly a good impression – but not to the initiated and intelligent members of the audience. The rub is that a man may possess these three qualities to the full, but on his feet, before an audience of strangers or critical colleagues, he can easily conceal or even destroy them.

Sincerity is revealed by being natural – such a simple thing in theory but often so difficult to carry out as you wrestle to master nervous tension. Showing, at the right time, the proper amount of enthusiasm and vitality; being assured in manner and voice because of the grasp you have of the subject; your spontaneous reaction to any incident (from an interruption by a member of the audience to your knocking over your cards) – each will reveal it.

If you are sincere, an audience will forgive you almost anything. Soon after the First World War, half the Queen's Hall orchestra used to play every other Sunday evening in winter at a town hall in London. Greeting them at the first visit of one season, a well-loved mayor spoke of 'this well known concert party'! There was an abrupt painful silence throughout the packed hall, and his face quickly matched the colour of his red robes. Then suddenly it beamed out into a huge smile, taken up in his voice – 'This orchestra, I mean this orchestra' – and the audience and players immediately relaxed and smiled, almost aloud, with him. Because he was a sincere man, he was quite forgiven.

How can sincerity be destroyed? Slickness of manner; bonhomie run riot; bluffing your way through – are all fair examples.

How can it be concealed? If you are flustered as you are about to speak you may fail to show sincerity. If, for instance, you are upset by arriving late, by, for the moment, mislaying your notes or by a bleak reception by the organisers, you will have to grapple with this feeling. The fault and the cure, in other circumstances, may lie in the hands of the chairman. A curt chairman may put a speaker on his feet before he has had time to sense the atmosphere; and if the speaker is inexperienced or sensitive by nature, this will suffice to fluster him. A good chairman, with no show of condescension, will size up the speaker and, if he shows any nervousness, ease him in with the audience – by the soothing tone of his voice and the choice of his words; without being long-winded, by talking at sufficient length for the speaker to see the audience coming into focus as individual normal human beings. Particularly if the chairman can judge his introduction so that the audience relaxes into a smile – not laughter – should the speaker's fluster be over.

Again, if you feel frustrated in groping to remember a speech you cannot show your sincerity. Frustration arises either because you have prepared the speech badly, or prepared it fully but at the last moment. In each case you are apt to be looking backward over your shoulder, as it were, feeling for your brief – and the forward drive, essential for all natural speaking, has gone.

Given the occasion, speak from the heart as well as from the head. Let your audience see how you feel as well as what you know. Remember an audience itself has a heart before a head. This requires self-discipline and sensitivity. An appeal to the intellect must always be the main approach, but on countless occasions, when persuasion for a good cause is needed, after the facts have been given an appeal to the emotions comes into its own. It may be a great national occasion in the Commons, or, a plea in support of some charity or national disaster; it may be a plea in the simpler circumstances of business policy or the work of a parochial church council. If the speech is of real importance, treat each member of the audience as if he or she is a missionary, eager, therefore, to do what you lucidly explain.

Friendliness begets friendliness. It does not mean a permanent veneer of smiling without meaning; 'claptrapping' your way through a speech; or smiling perpetually to attract sympathy, as an insurance policy against making a poor speech. Like the other two qualities, it must be a natural one. It particularly illustrates the direct connection between the eye and the voice. A twinkle in the eye automatically causes a twinkle in the voice. Friendliness, therefore, apparent in this dual way, is a lubricant to mellow solemnity to pleasant seriousness and to carry through dull facts enjoyably. It is the quality that must predominate at after-dinner speeches – so very much more important than the telling of a joke. It fits in with the relaxed mood of the guests, and, as just hinted, it allows of a serious contribution being included without the light-hearted manner being lost. Friendliness, as befits one of the three great qualities, in varying degree must be present in all speeches.

It is shown not only by the expression in the eyes but by the lines around them and the general change in features in keeping with what you are saying. It is shown by the modulation of the voice, the informality, from time to time, of your language and, not least, by the relaxed yet alert poise of the body. More particularly does it come into its own in the slight pause you should make between the main points – a pause of one or two seconds when you should look over the audience whilst they are digesting what has been said. Such a pause accompanied by a friendly look in the eye is but an enlargement of what you do when explaining a problem to a companion in private conversation – and yet it is a hallmark of a good speaker.

How do you destroy friendliness? Not to look at the audience is a splendid start. An unnecessarily loud voice and florid phrases both help. Tension, physical or mental, makes it impossible to be friendly, and in fact is inclined to affect the audience in similar manner. A man standing very taut, a hand tightly grasping a wrist across his body and a stern look on his face, deceives no thinking member of the audience. Another cause of destruction is lack of interest by the speaker – for example, a pompous politician, in measured pace, addressing his constituents – 'What would you like me to talk about next?'

But *the* clue to speaking is authority. You cannot command in speaking, you can only persuade. The fable of Aesop where the North Wind and the Sun compete to make a man remove his cloak illustrates this. Boreas blows more and more strongly, but the man draws his cloak more and more tightly to his body. Then the Sun shines more and more warmly and, by persuasion, the man removes the garment.

Yet it is to the Bible – to the New Testament – that we must turn to appreciate the full strength of this quality.

'For He taught them as one who had authority.'

The strength has been taken out of what Christ said by the passing of time; the repetition of the pulpit; the fairy-like dilution for childhood days; and the handicap of gathering together books of such variety into one volume, the Bible, badly arranged, unsuitably laid out for reading with pleasure, and often badly printed. But looked at afresh, much of His speaking is breathtaking in its wit and its authority; in the power it had to be understood and to strike home to rich and poor alike. Read the gospels in J. B. Phillips' modern English; read Dorothy Sayers' play-cycle, *The Man Born to be King,* with its outstanding and pungent introduction and notes – and this is clearly apparent. One can only hope the Aramaic in which Christ spoke helped His authority as good spoken English helps ours today.

Authority is attained by the interlocking of all the positive principles mentioned in this book – quality of fact and thought, of language, of delivery, all stamped by the speaker's personality. Hence, whilst sincerity and friendliness may be shown satisfactorily at an early stage, authority matures more gradually with experience. Again, unlike the other two, authority is a blend of two further qualities – conviction and intelligence.

Conviction will be revealed, for example, by your showing that you really believe what you are saying is interesting and important; more particularly, by your disclosing that it is the result of your personal thinking and feeling. Conviction will be gravely weakened by letting the argument meander; quite successfully destroyed by not looking at the audience. (It is not possible to exaggerate the importance of looking at your listeners when you speak. Ask a friend to stand in front of you and speak a sentence or so demanding authority. Let him do this first his eyes cast down, and then correctly looking at or towards you. To look at others as you speak is just good manners.)

Intelligence will be shown, for example, by speaking from your own experience and your own observation; by the range of your voice and the choice of your language. You will conceal it by speaking in generalities, particularly if you employ well used phrases.

It is fitting to conclude this chapter with a word on nervousness; for this more than anything can put the three essential qualities at risk. The bubble of nervous tension has been pricked early in chapter 1. There, strategy to cope with this perpetual challenge is suggested. It remains to consider a few tactics.

Before an important speech, try to have a few minutes complete bodily relaxation. If not immediately before, have it at least before you set out; and hang on to this detached spirit of ease ideally until your speech is over. To lie flat on the back for a few minutes, allowing all the muscles to relax, is a wonderful restorative, at all times, of bodily ease and balance of mind. (Sir Winston Churchill, through the more active part of his public life, paid tribute to the value of the siesta – learned by him as an observer of the Cuban guerilla war against Spain – by retiring to bed for a while after lunch.) Remember that speaking is a deed. Whilst you are waiting to speak, sit upright and well poised; at the same time, strive to relax all the muscles surrounding the lungs – and be sure the shoulders and arms are not taut.

If you are nervous before starting, sit well, as just described, and take a deliberate and fairly deep breath. Hold it for about five seconds and then breathe out slowly as *deeply* as you can, until you feel hollow at the bottom of the chest. Repeat this three or four times. Normally you will be doing this whilst you are being introduced. If the features and the body in general remain relaxed and if you move the head slightly, no one will notice what you are doing. Nervous tension makes you empty yourself of air; by increasing the supply of oxygen, the deep and slow breathing soothes you down.

If you feel on edge at the actual opening, start the speech with deliberate slowness for about one minute. Then, as you begin to feel a liaison with the audience, move smoothly to your normal pace. They can bear just about this amount of time of slow speaking, but no longer. To start too fast when nervous can be fatal. It is almost impossible to slow down; on the contrary, the tendency is to go faster and faster until an embarrassing gabble results. Only some outside interference can save you. (Those fortunate enough to know the novels of John Buchan will recall in *John Macnab* how

Sir Archibald Roylance was saved at a key meeting when he started to gibber by his servant, from the back of the large hall, roaring at him to speak up.)

One sign of nervousness is a dry mouth, which is not an advantage when you are speaking. If no water has been provided and it is too late to ask for it, drop the chin slightly and just open the mouth. In twenty to twenty-five seconds, saliva should return. A trial run looking at yourself in the mirror will convince you that you do not look absurd.

A speaker can be in full stride and suddenly break down and dry up. It may be simple forgetfulness; it may be he is so tense that his energy evaporates. In either case he must 'put on an act', such as filling his glass with water and having a drink, or taking out his handkerchief to blow his nose. Do such acts deliberately, so that you can think; the brain is capable of rapid recovery.

Remember that nervous tension is no monopoly of beginners. Experienced speakers, realising that they have a great challenge to meet, can falter. Speaking on television – a very specialised form of public speaking – persons of known skill and integrity, from time to time, are clearly ill at ease. Actors and actresses, in varying degrees, retain their feeling of meeting a challenge throughout the run of a play. They may even artificially encourage a nip of nervousness if they feel too complacent, so as to make sure that they will give of their best. Sir Ralph Richardson was on record a few years back as saying 'What makes you a professional is that you are used to being afraid. You accept fear'. Lord Birkett, up to his last case before going on the bench, had a degree of nervous tension – until he was on his feet.

Some degree of nervous tension must remain with a good speaker *always*. You must learn to harness the asset. To aim to be without it would mean that you had deadened a priceless quality.

6 Delivery – Stance, Gesture and Expression

A boxer depends on first class footwork throughout his bout – he boxes also with his legs. A sprinter depends on a balanced strong arm action throughout his race – he runs also with his arms. Similarly a speaker should depend on the gentle movement of his body, the smooth restraint of his gestures and, above all, on the expression in his eyes and on his features. All are irrefutably linked with the voice; it is no question of their being unco-ordinated adjuncts (hence the nonsense of suggesting that notes should be marked 'here make a gesture').

Such co-ordination is so rare firstly because we fail to realise that public speaking is simply an enlargement of a responsible conversation between two, in which one member monopolises the talking; and secondly, because we do not understand nervous tension. For each of us, without thought, shows this co-ordination in our everyday talk – asking for the marmalade at breakfast, stressing a point in committee, or chatting with friends. The kindly but blunt-speaking woman cleaner shooing away a dog lapping up water from her pail, and the workman in the public bar seeing his precious drink in peril of being knocked over – both speak with their eyes and their faces, their bodies and their arms, as well as with their voices. The business man need have no fear, in accepting such training, that he is being made into an actor.

Co-ordination not only makes you appear natural to the audience; it also makes you speak physically so much more easily. As explained in the next chapter, it helps your breathing and the modulation of the voice.

The key to holding yourself well is the simple but con-trasting phrase 'relaxed authority'. A great middle distance runner may appear to be making no effort because he knows how to relax; his back will be straight but his torso will not be taut, and each leg, as it finishes its stride, will momentarily rest as it comes forward for the next. A batsman or a golfer, before he shapes to hit the ball, stands with relaxed alert-ness. A boxer sparring for an opening holds himself likewise. If you prefer a more gentle analogy, an artist putting the finishing touches to a painting will stand upright yet relaxed to ensure perfect steadiness of his hand.

Standing like a guardsman on parade – at attention or at ease (such an absurd expression) – tautens the nervous system. The centre of this system is at the base of the spine, from where, right up the stiffly held back, runs the spinal cord. The hand starts to grip the wrist tautly; the chest stiffens; the eyes either glare, or glaze; and the voice betrays the tension. Such strong-man appearance is very brittle. Experienced mem-bers of the audience will not be deceived, whilst sensitive members will feel some of this tenseness affecting them and will not like it. It is unnatural to keep quite still. Sentry duty is not fun; standing in the corner as a dunce has this element of punishment in it.

Stand easy and upright, the stomach in, the chest well held, the head well poised and the feet comfortably apart. *Keep the feet still.* Then, as you speak, turn smoothly from left to right, using all the joints given you for this purpose – the ankles, the knees, the hips and the shoulders. Particu-larly give the head – smoothly – the fuller mobility it com-mands through the top two bones of the vertebral column, the atlas and the axis, allowing it to move sideways, upwards and downwards, forwards and, if need be, backwards. Traversing the audience in this way is such a natural action. The host wel-coming his guests at an official function; the managing direc-tor, standing in front of the mantelpiece a little apologetic for calling a board meeting at a highly inconvenient time; the colonel warming his back at the fire awaiting visitors on guest night – all automatically swing their bodies round to face and greet their visitors (also expressing in their eyes and on their features their welcome).

Traversing in this natural way also greatly helps you, the speaker. It allows too much nervous tension – or too much nervous energy – a healthy outlet. Tension that might have been shown in fidgeting, gesturing far too much or dancing around on the feet, is used up unnoticeably.

If you hold the legs close together – perhaps seeking greater confidence thereby – movement is distinctly cramped. You can turn only like a butler presenting a card on a tray; or you feel a relationship to a performing seal or the minute celluloid figures with round metal bases that come out of Christmas crackers. Be sure to keep the feet well apart and still. Certainly twitch the toes, if you wish. By all means, occasionally shift your ground – say, every five minutes – but do so unhurriedly. There must never be any unnecessary movement of feet, arms, hands or face.

Initially, to master all the points that make up 'relaxed authority' – to gain poise – stand on a hard chair, and speak to an imaginary audience.

If you speak sitting down – by custom of the meeting, through injury or illness, when answering questions after a speech – do sit well. Authority remains essential. Get your 'tail' well back, keep the stomach in and the back straight. Let the body lean slightly forward from the hips. This position of relaxed authority is not only for appearance but, as always, for good breathing and the comfort of your throat.

Guard particularly against habits. Unless the speaker and his subject are outstanding, audiences of every variety are easily distracted. The speaker who sniffs regularly, who constantly touches his nose, or who keeps on lining up his cards; the lawyer in court who is always taking his glasses on and off; the member of the House of Lords who 'puts it to their lordships' by windmilling his glasses round in outstretched hand; the lecturer who takes up the gavel and toys with its removable head; the Member of Parliament, of some years ago, who used to pat the top of his thigh bone and pull on his shirt until all present had but one purpose, to await the appearance of the tail – all distract their listeners.

Watch as well personal appearance. Be neither showy nor untidy. A waistcoat which is a walking advertisement for an association of wallpaper manufacturers, or a feminine hat too exotic in look; in contrast, a tie whose knot is sheltering under one corner of a dishevelled collar, or a windblown crop of hair – each distracts (and may even prejudice) the audience, and so takes away the vital authority of the speech.

Secondly, the use of the hands is most important. If a suspect is an old lag, he may, by the expression of his eyes and features in general be able to brazen his way out. But if he is not quite in this class, the detective may notice that his hands, held by his side, are twitching. Accordingly, hands are of importance to the speaker first for the damage they can do. Never clasp them together, or hold a wrist, tightly. Artificial control reveals tension – and can actually stiffen the expression. In contrast, do not let them flit about – behind the back for a few seconds, then on to the table or into the pockets or clasped around the body. Yet, properly used, movement of the hands is part of our expression of thought. All of us use our hands to some degree in conversation. We should do precisely the same when speaking in public, being sure that we keep quite natural.

If you are a little taut, why not start with the hands *lightly* clasped behind the back? Hold the body, as always, well – like the stand-at-ease position, but both arms and trunk relaxed. This is a natural stance and the arms can come forward quite smoothly to gesture.

The best position of all is the cradling of the hands just under the ribs, akin to the holding of hands in Communion – the right hand gently resting in the left palm with the left thumb locking both together. The body seems in complete balance. The quiet gesture to the left and to the right; the simultaneous gesture to each side, or the shrug of the shoulders as the hands move out, all seem so natural. The lock of the left thumb keeps the hands in repose from fidgeting (clasping them palm to palm is all right when you are experienced, but before that it may result in your rubbing them together like a street vendor).

The hands clasped across the crutch is another alternative; but be sure not to become pigeon-breasted (in all positions, the body should constantly be well held).

Hands held by the side at arm's length, the backs showing slightly, fit a quiet speaker, or a quiet passage in a speech.

Hands in the coat pockets give a pleasant relaxed stance, but again beware of becoming pigeon-breasted – like a man pocketing and aiming two revolvers. On the other hand, do not roll the hands about, like a pair of ferrets anxious to go into action. One hand in the pocket is equally effective. With one exception, never put the hand in the trousers' pocket – it looks too casual. But when wearing tails or a morning coat, a hand slipped into a trouser pocket contrasts with the dignity of the dress. Be sure your coat pockets let you easily remove the hands to gesture, and for this purpose, if not for general appearance, it is better to keep the coat unbuttoned, particularly if you are wearing a double-breasted jacket.

Be most careful how you use the table. To touch it with the hands without leaning, the outstretched fingers gently making contact, is a sound position. However, very easily a nervous or thoughtless speaker emulates the stance of a duck, which, as stated in chapter 3, is not only ugly, but it means either that you commit the sin of not looking at the audience and also crease the throat, or, by stretching up to look, you put serious strain on over-stretched vocal cords. Again, if you are nervous, at the least you may stiffen the hands and fingers, like the bones of a skate, or, at the other extreme, you may start playing the piano over the table.

Holding cards – *half* cards – to nestle in the palm of the hand, is an excellent position. Keep them snuggled across and below the ribs; and remember to lift them *forward and up* when referring to them.

The distaff side, very unfairly, has not so many alternative positions as the male. But first as to stance, a woman needs to stand just as comfortably, her feet apart so she can traverse the audience; yet she may like to place one foot slightly forward, thus giving the body less 'head-on' appearance. Hands behind the back or in the pockets, if they exist, each seems at least aesthetically out of consideration. Yet four or five positions remain. Hands gently clasped under the ribs – the under or over-clasp – is the best position of all. If the dangers are firmly remembered, resting the finger tips on the table – so there is no sign of inner tension – looks very graceful for a woman. Holding half-cards, tucked in the hollow of the ribs, often meets admirably the many social occasions when a woman has to speak. Then, particularly if the 'one-shouldered stance' is agreed to, to rest one hand on a shaped firm handbag has practical elegance. Another variation when using half-cards for notes is for the spare hand lightly to grasp the wrist – and then, if you wish, this grip can be retained as you lift the notes forward and up for reference. In this last instance, the cards may have to be held just a fraction higher, and, when you raise them, you will not be able to hold them as far away as in the normal grip.

During a speech, of course, change the position of the hands occasionally if you wish; but always smoothly, naturally.

It is natural from the hands to move, thirdly, to gestures, made by the hands and arms in combination. Gestures, helped by the features, may have been the first form of communication – when breathing, and eating and drinking were the only functions of the mouth and surrounding parts of the body. They serve to emphasise, as do the momentary changes of pace, power and pitch of the voice (essentially aided by the disciplined rein of the pause). They are made in complete co-ordination with the modulation of the voice. In this respect, a speaker is like a musician conducting himself. Stand quite still, head not moving and arms by the sides, and make an emphatic point in speaking – 'I think this action is *disgraceful*'. You will feel a thump in the diaphragm – the strong gristly muscle lying at the bottom of the lungs. The slightest gesture of the arm, or even the hand (or a slight move of the head) completely removes this thump.

Gesture with moderation — in size and in number. The eyes and the expression on the face or the slight movement of the head may suffice. In view of what has been said in the beginning, of the smooth links between body, gesture, expression and voice, such movements will always be spontaneous. Be sure that they are smooth and relaxed. Here we differ from the creature and bird worlds. The tree rat in Richmond Park and the song thrush in Kensington Gardens, although both graceful in movement, dart and jerk when they are standing on one spot (obeying the two primitive rules of Nature, 'to eat' and 'not to be eaten'). Any suggestion of exaggerated movement, like that of so many at 'Speakers' Corner' in Hyde Park, must be avoided. Again, never hold an 'attitude' — such as a spreading wide of the arms.

Always make gestures outwards, from the centre of the body. Mr Harold Macmillan, when prime minister, acknowledging an audience as he arrived at a large meeting would swing both arms outwards from his sides above his head — like a boxer before a fight, or an umpire at cricket signalling a hit for six — but he would not dream of doing so during a speech.

Important as are the poise of the body — in stance and gentle movement — and the smooth, restrained use of the hands and arms, the look in the eyes and the corresponding expression of the face are of even greater importance. In life, the eyes show all the ranges of feeling — love and hate, anger and joy, kindness, compassion, lust, fear, surprise, sincerity, friendliness and authority. It is the last three that in the discipline of speaking in public are the most prominent.

Four tests prove the complete co-ordination between voice and eye. Firstly, a fundamental of speaking is that where the eyes look the voice carries. The voice, is, as it were, aimed by the eyes. Hence you should speak most of the time looking to those at the back (keeping the voice in the same pitch and power as you traverse those in the centre and the front). Like all rules this has to be interpreted reasonably, but on the turn of the century, when Churchill entered Parliament, members successfully addressed meetings of 5-6,000 by applying this rule.

Secondly, look in the mirror as angrily as possible, and try to speak happily. It is impossible to do so until the features and eyes relax to disclose happiness. Then look in the mirror, the features wreathed in smiles and try and speak angrily – the principle holds.

But if a speaker is blind, his eyelids closed, then surely the principle falls? Try yourself – and also get an experienced speaker to demonstrate to you. The features take up all the feeling and expression of the hidden eyes, reflecting the rhythm of the voice and conveying your personality still to the audience.

Finally, as good a test as any, is that just mentioned in discussing gestures. Similarly a movement of the head, emphasised by the chin, removes the thump from the diaphragm.

The importance of the eyes and the features in speaking was stressed in chapter 5.

Be sure to stand back well from your notes – a yard is a reasonable measure to have in mind – so that the eyes approximately line up with them and with the centre or the back of the audience. The notes must be well set out and clearly written. Constant dipping down towards them, by breaking the contact with the audience, removes authority.

Check your general poise as you are about to speak. Keep relaxed like the athlete of class or the artist putting the finishing touches to his picture; but below the surface there should be an air of alert anticipation and of friendly command. Then, as mentioned in chapter 2, as the applause begins, rise up smoothly. When it ceases, do not at once begin to speak. Wait at least three seconds (if you wish, count to yourself 'one and two and three') whilst feet cease to scuffle and dresses to rustle. Then swing through the hips slightly towards the chairman and bow your acknowledgement, equally slightly, obviously having a friendly expression on the face; swing towards the far left corner and say 'Mr Chairman'; and finally to the far right corner and say 'Ladies and Gentlemen'. The pausing before speaking and then between the 'salutation' are important to give a friendly dignity. Ensure too your physical action is smooth. When you become confident, you may choose, during the three seconds' pause, to look naturally over the audience. Until then, either keeping the head bowed or looking over the top of the audience – in prolongation of your attitude during the period of applause – will give you greatest ease. If you are a little on edge, draw on your sense of humour to smile at yourself. The suggestion of speaking all the words towards the audience ensures that the very first words are not muffled, and that when you have to use a standing microphone, with its limited arc of traverse, every word will be heard.

The last paragraph implies that you are quite ready when you rise – like the batsman who has taken accurate guard and looked carefully around the field before facing the bowler. Before the chairman introduces you is the time, if necessary, to clear the throat and adjust the tie. Certainly this is the time to lay down your watch and, standing up temporarily for the purpose, to be sure your notes are well placed in height and distance for light. Otherwise your approach, your vital introduction can resemble a hen scratching around.

A particular fault of so many speakers is to glance at their notes directly they have acknowledged the chairman and audience – so breaking the current as soon as contact has been made. You must know what you propose saying at the very start of the speech; this is merely a nervous habit that can take the edge off a good first impression. This is cousin to the habit of looking at the notes too quickly after making your important points, instead of continuing to look at the audience for a second or so.

There should always be a quality of restrained energy behind a good speaker, a reserve of power, as it were; but keep it in hand. In speaking we are appealing to the ear. Reliable psychologists say that most people's knowledge comes from visual impression. Be sure, therefore, that your presentation

E

in poise, gesture and expression does not distract from your effort.

To realise the need of this complete co-ordination of voice, stance, gesture and expression – yet to appreciate its natural-ness – watch television with the sound turned off. Choose a well cast play at one extreme, a responsible discussion at the other. Having rightly concentrated on the voices to under-stand what is happening, you will now appreciate how the ex-pression of the eyes and face and the gentle movement of the body and the hands instinctively link in with the words.

Remember to retain your poise of relaxed authority in the conclusion. So many speakers wilt in an apologetic way at this crucial stage. In fact, do not be so relaxed in bearing; and in the tone of voice and the expression of face indicate the curtain is about to be rung down. As you end, pause a second, and then bow slightly to the audience before sitting down.

7 Delivery – The Voice

'No instrument can be made to compete, in variety and significance of expression, with the cultured human voice naturally used.' Harley Granville-Barker, the stage director and dramatist, had foremost in mind the actor speaking the word music of Shakespeare. 'Cultured' too is a word that halts the man of affairs in his tracks. Politics, from Hitler to Mao, has given 'culture' a false and tragic meaning. Even in the arts themselves nowadays it fosters much pretence both among the executants and their audiences. And, as stated, in its own right meaning it has always jarred the practical man whose imagination must, of necessity, be disciplined. Yet he would be foolish to ignore the value of a good voice 'naturally used'; the instrument through which he reveals his well planned facts and thoughts, his chosen language and his personality.

It is not in the least unmanly to have a well modulated voice – if one remains natural. This is not the monopoly of the educated. For example, a Welsh farmhand and a Glaswegian waitress often speak clear attractive English. On the other hand, because a man has inherited a well sounding voice it does not necessarily mean that he is going to use it to best advantage. Just as, if he is given a priceless 'Stradivarius' and cannot play it the instrument will remain but an interesting museum piece, so, in lesser but similar vein, if he has a good voice but has no idea how to modulate it then it remains a wasted asset.

The change in the voice, after good tuition and patient practice, should not be so obvious as to cause open comment; but you must have the determination and the sense of humour to stand up to reasonable comment. In the process of improving your speaking it is essential to remain natural, and this itself should ensure that any remarks which are passed should be favourable. It is quite wrong to feel any embarrassment or any excessive shyness. Such a feeling could prohibit the desired change, even kill it at birth; you would be stifling the very object you had striven to achieve. A man after taking lessons in golf always likes friends to notice the improvement in his skill. Although voice training is a more personal matter, let the result at least speak for itself.

Modulation does not entail the acquiring of a standardised voice. As to the acquisition of a BBC accent, apparently the ambition of several, it should be remembered that the announcers are *reading* aloud not speaking, and even so, some do it well and some indifferently. The English 'public school' accent is basically very good – as also was that once known as the 'Oxford' accent. It is spoiled by the few who exaggerate in a disagreeably affected way the suffix '-ly', or the vowel 'O', or bid someone or some animal 'Come heah!'

It is such a pity that the teaching profession does not have the simple tuition required to fit all its members, as they go about their everyday work, to give an example of natural good speaking, and to fit those specially gifted to instruct all the pupils in this basic human quality. As has been said earlier, English is the loveliest and most expressive of languages. To appreciate it only in writing is to miss most of its glory. The rub is that difference in speech, in the use of the voice – and also, it is true, in the use of the language – is the most obstinate survival of class distinction. If schoolchildren throughout the day were set such an example so that good natural speaking became a habit with them, and if at some well chosen stage they were given definite lessons by one dedicated to the strength and beauty of the language and sensitive to each child being a different personality – great good could result.

The danger of some children being mocked in their homes by the grown-ups could be offset partly by the knowledge that all children were the subject of such influence; partly by sensible liaison of the teachers with the parents, explaining

> . . . and at his heels,
> Leash'd in like hounds, should famine, sword and fire
> Crouch for employment.

>   Many a time and oft
> Have you climbed up to walls and battlements,
> To towers and windows, yea, to chimney-tops,

> . . . for in the very torrent, tempest, and, as I may
> say, whirlwind of your passion, . . .

To raise the pitch once or twice during a speech on the introductory word or short phrase of a new argument is excellent speaking. This being a new part of the speech, the pause beforehand will be quite long. Pause deliberately afterwards as well; perhaps introduce a short question. ('Sanctions . . . . what of sanctions?') This higher pitch, good pausing and the question in the voice can rivet the attention of the audience.

The third quality is change of power. Normally, we emphasise a word or syllable by an increase in power. Used occasionally, to achieve surprise, speaking more quietly can be very effective. Speak a simple phrase in both ways ('I think this is *incredible*'). Notice that in both methods you do not only change the power of the voice. In each case, if you are speaking well, you depend on a pause before the emphasised syllable. Secondly, in an increase of power there is an increase of pace; in a decrease of power there is a decrease of pace. This alternative, of speaking more quietly for emphasis, is unrivalled in a conversational style of talking – such as answering questions in normal public speaking, and any speaking on television or radio.

Your general power of speech will be gauged as soon as you arrive at the meeting by your noting the size of the audience and the acoustics of the place. As to the latter, if you have any doubts have a word with the manager or the chairman before the meeting starts. In any case, always bear in mind the basic rule 'where the eyes look the voice carries' and in the opening sentences watch the reaction of those at the back. Are their faces strained, are they leaning forward; or, are they looking a little overwhelmed? If the meeting is so large that you cannot clearly see those furthest away (and you have no microphone), then by all means ask them before you start – 'Can you hear me?' Do this only on such a rare occasion, otherwise the audience may feel you do not know your job.

Two cardinal faults are associated with the power of delivery – dropping the voice at the end of a sentence, or, more abruptly, just biting off the end of a word. Ours may be the loveliest of languages, but it has one handicap – rarely is the last syllable of a word stressed. (This is one reason why Italian opera, written in words so often ending in vowels, suffers by translation into English.) The more interesting your speech, the more sorry an audience is at losing the concluding words. The cure for this fault is to dam up the breath, to pause, before the last word or syllable. Then the release of the breath gives an added strength so that you can either heighten your pitch or increase your power. This is but another application – a practical application – of emphasis, which is mentioned in the next two paragraphs. Behind this skill lies the permanent ability to throw the voice forward to the front of the mouth where the sound hits the hard palate above and behind the teeth.

Last, there is pausing, which requires mention in three contexts. Firstly, an indication in a long speech that you are pausing for a few seconds – by quietly sipping some water, or by your general manner relaxing – is appreciated by an audience. They can change their posture, murmur to their neighbours and generally relax their attention. Secondly, there is the very important type of pause, already mentioned, made regularly throughout a speech, when, after making your main points, you hold the audience with a friendly look whilst they digest them. But the pause that matters in this chapter is that made to achieve emphasis : the pause before, and often after, a word or syllable to make it stand out. Such pauses are the key to clear and significant speaking (and how much easier they will make speaking for you). From this launching pad comes the essential control of the other three qualities — the changes in pace, in pitch and in power. Pausing provides the vital asset, breath control. Remember that pausing is part of speaking; for a pause is a silence *implying* sound.

In what other ways is emphasis achieved? It is accomplished by a combination of two or more of the four qualities of voice, essentially accompanied by a change of expression, probably by some movement of the head, and perhaps by a gesture.

Proper breathing is essential to good speaking. It controls the modulation of the voice; it provides capacity and stamina for speaking at length, or for addressing a large audience unaided by the microphone. So many people breathe badly. So many appear never to have used their full breathing apparatus and always nip their breath only from the upper part of the lungs. Many women, possibly because of their more restrictive clothing, remain in this respect particularly bad offenders. The breath should be a deep upward movement, coming right up from the diaphragm, the large muscle sealing off the lungs from the internal organs.

Be sure that you carry the head well, so that the muscles of the throat are not restricted. As a basic position, tilt the head very slightly forward and downward. Remember (chapters 3 and 6) that leaning the body by placing the hands on the table, apart from its potential ugliness, makes you either crease the throat, so dulling your delivery, or in your effort to look at the audience, tauten the throat, so causing great strain, perhaps hoarseness that will last quite a time.

Remember that the voice is 'aimed' by the eyes, and accordingly speak most of the time to those furthest away. Bear in mind that you should be traversing the audience eighty to ninety per cent of the time that you are speaking. When you have completed a main point you must not at once glance at your notes, but continue to look over the audience for a second or more. This is such a natural, courteous act in normal conversation, but the desire to press on means that this pause is very often neglected in public speaking. It registers goodwill; you cannot but look with friendliness. It gives the listeners time to digest what you have said. This pausing is one of the finer points of speaking, and its use should be assiduously practised if you wish to be a good speaker. As is so often the case in carrying out the principles of this art, you also benefit; it is so much easier to speak assisted by such pausing.

If you wish to read an extract from, say, a newspaper or a government report, obey three rules. Firstly, do not obscure the face; hold the document breast high and, in the usual fashion, well away from you. Secondly, show a natural contrast in your intonation – you are now reading. Above all, you must traverse the audience about thirty per cent of the time that you are reading, so that you retain authority over them. This habit is easy to acquire by practice, whilst the mere fact of traversing lets the eyes run across the notes. Also have faith that the eyes will go back to where you last looked.

Recollect that the speech of the best speakers in public hardly differs in principle from that used in their family circle, which illustrates so vividly the fundamental, that speaking in public is merely a disciplined enlargement of a responsible conversation. As you strive, but always with enjoyment, to improve your delivery, through every stage keep *natural;* guard particularly against a false gentility. Remember that the rhythm and the meaning of words are interlocked, and that the speaker has the priceless advantage over the writer that the inflexion of his voice can show this to the full. Be careful to avoid the habit of so many of the clergy of 'surging' loudly, quite out of relation to the modulation or the emphasis required. The cause of this seems partly a belief that 'unnatural' speaking is necessary in God's presence, partly to encourage themselves when the congregation appears inattentive. This habit remains also, from time to time, amongst many of the older trade union leaders. Many of those reading out sports results on radio also 'surge'. Theirs is not an easy task when governed by time, but correct breathing and the knowledge of how to modulate the voice properly would stop this elementary fault.

We cannot hear our own voices correctly. To start with the ears are behind the mouth. We hear rather the re-bound of the sound. What we hear comes mainly from the vibration in the bones of the head – the reflected sound thrown back (and slightly distorted). But the sounds of speech vibrate not only the parts going to make up the voice but *all* the bones of the head and many of the body. Borrow your doctor's stethoscope, apply it to your knee and you will hear the vibration of your speech. With this experience in mind, imagine the effect of speech on the small bones of your ears. You can have some idea how your voice sounds to others by cupping a hand around one ear, pushing the ear forward whilst turning the head to help; nowadays, a complete idea by the use of a good tape recorder.

In many other languages it is the enunciation of the vowels that is important. In English it is the articulation of the consonants. Yet, having it both ways, it is the vowels that give us our tonal beauty. 'L' is our most liquid and most beautiful consonant ('The lilting of the lute lingers long'). Be careful of the sibilants, the hissing sounds – 's', 'sh' – particularly when coming at the end of a word. 'Over-sibilance' should be avoided as much as possible, especially when speaking on radio or television.

8 Delivery – Exercises for the Voice

To attain and then to keep a voice which is authoritative and friendly, and which is well modulated and resonant requires constant practice. Yet the self-discipline and patience which are necessary are so worthwhile, and the time involved is short. It is regularity of exercise that is important. Many varieties of exercise are used at the many schools of drama; some can also be borrowed or adapted from the many schools of music. However, to ensure that this essential quality of a good speech blends with the other three qualities (well chosen facts and ideas, simple language and natural personality) and to put the cut and thrust of speaking in business, in professional and in political life on a high level, three or four simple exercises should suffice. Because they are simple they should not be scamped; most important issues in life are simple. All training has a certain dullness, otherwise it would not have the essential ingredients of discipline – it is the reward that matters. This is the spirit which drives the boxer punching the light and heavy bags, the cricketer and the golfer practising their strokes and the ballet dancer keeping lissom.

A resonant voice is within the grasp of nearly everybody. It is associated almost invariably with modulation. But a man may have a voice like a nutmeg grater, yet by appreciating the use of the momentary change of pace, of pitch and of power, and of good pausing he can still speak with authority. Although he has no suggestion of resonance, he is able to command inflexion of language. People normally lack resonance of voice because they do not make full use of the lungs and the many resonant cavities of the head and upper body; because the jaw muscles have become rigid, the mouth has become tight and the tongue physically lazy.

Humming is the key exercise. Hum on the letter 'M', which means that the lips to all intents and purposes are closed and you are using the post-nasal cavities. The word to have burnt into your brain all the time you are humming is 'forward!' Speaking from the front of the mouth is essential for good audibility; for the ability to carry your words to the farthest that your eyes must look; for an insurance against dropping the voice or biting off the end of words, and for sheer selfish ease of speaking. You strive to throw the sound forward particularly so as to use the hard palate which is the sounding board for the voice.

The proof that you are humming correctly is with you at the time. Very soon the inside of the lips, particularly of the upper lip, becomes warm. Probably it will tingle, rather like but not so pronounced as the outside of your lips used to when, as a child, you played on a comb covered in tissue paper. The tingling and the warmth, in that order, should be felt within a minute. Quality of humming is more important than volume.

When you have mastered the simple technique, then you can hum in odd moments. You can hum when you are strolling in the garden or stretching your limbs in the office; when you are walking through the noise of crowded streets or in the peace of a London square. You can hum when you are riding, like Lord Wavell speaking poetry aloud as in the early morning he rode over the plains of Delhi. You can hum when driving or held up in your car (but allow then for the fact that your posture is bad for perfect results).

Yet first go into a quiet room, stand with 'relaxed authority' and close the eyes so that you can concentrate on the sound. Hum in your normal pitch as quietly as you can, concentrating on holding the pitch and bringing the sound forward. Then, being most careful not to change the pitch, gradually increase the power. This mastered, increase and decrease the

power whilst still holding the constant pitch; for the exercise is also excellent for enlarging the capacity to breathe.
Repeat the exercise, still with the greatest care, first on a
lower then on a higher note. Help yourself to succeed by
visualising the stream of air ascending from the bottom of the
lungs to the lips.

Then occasionally let the lips very slightly open and close,
to test that they are held firmly but not tightly. This will
produce a 'm-m-m-m' sound. Later on, lessen the monotony
of simplicity by humming some music of a marked rhythm,
always with a deliberate beat, never with the casualness normally associated with everyday humming.

Most people do not throw the voice forward and several
speak right at the back of the throat; hence the special importance of this exercise. At first do it for three to four minutes
at a time; and when it is mastered strive to keep up the custom
for a couple of minutes daily. Be or become relaxed as you
practise it.

Complementary to this exercise is to hum up and down the
ordinary major scale. Do this with a deliberately slow but
smooth beat. Do not strain yourself, but try it gradually from
a low note, then from one slightly higher and carry on such
procedure until you find one most suitable to the compass
of your voice. This exercise shows up two blemishes common
to all too many – very poor breathing capacity and the
inability to change pitch. The latter is probably a quality lost
in childhood. A variation on this exercise, when it has been
mastered, is to hum a string of notes (the 'm-m-m-m' sound)
on each successive note of the chromatic scale.

Finally, leading on from the change of pitch when you are
humming, to say a word about tone deafness may be useful.
This term is used, it seems, to describe two different states.
There is the person who cannot *distinguish* between two
sounds as to pitch – similar to colour blindness. There is the
person who cannot control his vocal muscles and nerves so
as to *produce* the pitch of a note which he *hears* perfectly
well. It may go back to the time when the voice broke in

childhood. Some degree of control, then temporarily lost, may have become permanently so through, for example, not engaging whilst at school in singing. Putting a 'culprit' between two pupils who can sing, and telling him just to sing to himself until one day he is inspired to burst forth in unison, may do the trick. Actually, the production of a definite pitch in the voice is a complex affair. If a person can achieve correctly three or four notes of the scale then the trouble would seem to be of this secondary type – lack of neuro-muscular control, and not in any way an inability of hearing.

It is not much use disciplining a column of air to produce effective sound if the exit for it is unsuitable. The second exercise aims to make the lips flexible. It is no question of making the mouth large and ugly, but of taking away the tightness that comes with age, with facing life's problems too solemnly. Although the expressions to be seen are not particularly attractive, at least to start with, stand in front of a mirror. First stretch the lips horizontally, not violently but determinedly, ten to twelve times, letting the teeth, if they wish, open a little. Obtain the lift from below the nostrils, not from below the eyes. Then repeat the exercise humming 'eeee . . . .' – from the front of the mouth.

Secondly, purse together, round the lips as firmly as you can, visualising either the mouth of a sponge bag being drawn up tightly by its strings, or Kipling's account of how the Elephant's Child got its trunk. Really feel the lips being pulled, or rather, pushed forward. Later do this movement to the humming of 'ooh'. In its ejaculatory form this is a most natural sound ('Ooh! how *dare* you do that!').

Then physically link the two movements smoothly together. When satisfied that the vision seen is all that is desired, move equally smoothly into humming. The fact that this sound has recently been stolen, at least in the metropolis, by the police cars, should not distract you. This exercise achieves three objects – the firm stretching of the lips (its main purpose), the throwing forward of the sound and the improvement of the breathing. With some discretion, this exercise can also be done in the street and other open places – even if in tone 'sotto voce'.

The third exercise, save in the wide open spaces or in the dark, does demand some privacy. You poke out the tongue. Do not cheat, as in school, by pursing the lips around it. Open the mouth widely but not uncomfortably. In this case also you must stand in front of a mirror.

But first, what is the object of this exercise? If you have no tongue you cannot speak. If the tongue is not correctly attached to the floor of the mouth or to the throat at the back of the mouth, then you will speak with an impediment. Again, through its size or its shape, or even through your slovenliness in speaking, you may lisp. Compare the mouth and its tongue with the simplest of musical instruments, the tin whistle. Without the small dry pea, able to move about freely in its mouth, the whistle could play no tune.

When speech is necessary the tongue must not be allowed to lie flabbily and uselessly in the mouth. It must attack. It has a vital part to play in articulation in general and in skilled change of pace in particular. This third exercise is the most difficult for most people. Save with those having the ability to 'hole out in one', it is better attempted in two stages. The ultimate aim is to make the tongue dart, at great speed, in and out of the mouth. Visualise for comparison a boxer ratatatting with a straight left on a light bag, a mechanised battering ram in action, or a lizard, basking on a sunny rock, swiftly darting its long thin tongue out and in to catch an insect.

The tongue has to be gathered up for this purpose of smooth, fast and continuous 'striking'. You achieve this by pointing it – by sharpening its tip. First, keeping the mouth steadily open (remember this carefully throughout), glide the tip of the tongue so far as the teeth. Then, slowly and deliberately, with great concentration, push it forward, striving from the beginning to gather it up. Do not strain it at the root, or at the ligament attaching it to the lower mouth; but certainly feel a gentle yet firm pull at the root. For you are trying to loosen the tongue. Five or six attempts are sufficient before taking a short rest, for the exercise entails holding the breath and can be quite exhausting. Patience and, as with the other exercises, a sense of humour are essential, but the reward is worthwhile.

When sufficient progress is achieved, make the two parts into one exercise. Blend them slowly at the beginning, making sure as you increase your speed eventually to the maximum that the mouth remains constantly open. No sound accompanies this exercise. Do not overdo it. When starting, in two parts, five concentrated minutes, including pauses, is sufficient. Later, when adopted by you as a daily exercise, one minute is enough. Be careful that you do not make the underpart of the tongue sore as it passes over the lower teeth.

Some supplementary exercises deserve brief mention. If the lip exercises do not loosen the jaw muscles as effectively as wished, and you can afford it, try chewing some tacky toffee.

The lifting of the upper lip independently – in appearance rather like a bad tempered terrier starting to snarl – both strengthens and flexes it. As with the second main exercise, lift from the nostrils and not from the eyes.

Another exercise for the tongue, not so useful but easier, is to poke it out sufficiently to feel a gentle pull at the root, then swing it strongly from side to side. As in the main exercise, keep the mouth open and clear of the tongue.

A fourth minor exercise, for the flexibility of both the tongue and the lips – in which you can emulate the players of wind instruments – is to repeat rapidly a series of 't-t-t-t-t' or 'k-k-k-k-k' (or 'p-p-p-p-p'). These may have to be done slowly at first, but if kept up at a regular pace, will become easier.

Ours is not a nasal language. When someone does speak nasally, it is probably due either to the soft palate at the back of his throat becoming lazy, or his uneven breath control. Cure the first by keeping the mouth open and saying rapidly and repeatedly 'Ah-ng', or 'Oy-ng'. If you wish, say both in succession. In either case, be sure to throw the sound

F

forward. Cure the second fault by doing some deep breathing before an open window soon after rising.

In a more light-hearted yet still responsible way, try singing snatches of song. Choose the right moments so as not to jar the members of the family, or give any appearance of heartiness. Power is not essential; reserve it for selected occasions. The flexibility such singing can give, and the custom of hearing your voice in unfamiliar range can be of considerable value.

In the same mood, if you have military leanings, past or present, bugle calls predominantly hummed, but with sufficient breath allowed to escape through your puffed lips to play the tune, exercise the tongue splendidly and continue for you the practice of humming.

What causes speech? It is only a secondary function of the lungs to produce speech. We speak by means of breath which is being returned from the lungs – by means of exhaled air. The brain by impulse orders a sound, and a column of air is squeezed from the lungs and through the windpipe to the larynx, the 'voice box', resting at the top of the windpipe. (It is interesting to know that the original function of the larynx was simply as a muscle to protect the air passage by closing it against the entry of food, and so to enable breathing to continue whilst we swallowed. The production of noise in this throat cavity is an adaptive function.) In the 'box' are the vocal cords – two folds of tissue the vibration of which by this column of air creates the sound waves on which our voice is built. The cords vibrate at great speed – for example, in the case of a soprano singing, from around 250 to 850 times a second – but the sounds given off are too small to be easily heard by the human ear.

The pressure needed to squeeze this column of air is provided by the contraction of the muscles of the abdominal wall and of the upper part of the body, and particularly by the contraction of the diaphragm, the strong muscular partition separating these two parts of the trunk. Together, all these muscles provide a bellows-like action.

From the larynx the notes mount into the resonant cavities of the head. First, they enter the throat, where the back of the tongue, the soft palate above it, the back part of the nasal passages and the sidewalls of the throat itself reinforce their volume. Then they move to the cavity of the mouth where the mobility of the tongue, the curve of the teeth and the shaping of the lips bounce them off the hard palate – the sounding board for the voice. Meanwhile, the vibration caused above, in the sinuses around the nose, and below, in the great cavity of the chest, helps to bring the sounds to full maturity.

It is also in the cavities of the throat and the mouth that sound is moulded into speech – by the muscles of the throat, the palate, the cheeks, the tongue, the jaws and the lips; all aided by the teeth. The tongue plays a major part in the final stage, articulating all the sounds – the vowels and the consonants – acting as the main arbiter of pace and helping to move the sounds towards the hard palate.

If your throat is husky or your voice tired, gargle with a teaspoonful of salt, the right measure of glycerine of thymol or similar products in half a tumbler of warm water. If in trouble sometime before a meeting, frequent gargling can strengthen the voice.

One important discipline remains to be mentioned. The exercises suggested will give you the foundation of a well modulated voice, but to allow you to build on them – and in so doing perhaps to discover a new pleasure – you must acquire the habit of reading aloud, then speaking, good poetry. The value of poetry for the speaker has been stressed in chapter 4, dealing with language. Reading aloud, then speaking poetry combine three priceless merits. They inspire you with great and beautiful thoughts which can remain with you for ever. They can give you knowledge of, and so potential command of, language at its best. They can in the most enjoyable way, if you play your part, give you a fine voice.

In such reading aloud then speaking you will be in the most manly company. It is best always to start speaking quietly. Stand up or sit down, as you please. Speak a line or a thought, if need be, over and over again. Chisel your speaking – by pause, by change of pace, of pitch or of power – until you are satisfied with the result. Always speak to bring out the meaning, and not in individual words. When you have passed through the initial experiments, trying out different ways of speaking a line or a thought, start to look up as you near your final choice – as if you had an audience. And when you have reached it, look up and around as much as possible. Notice how the eyes and features, and occasionally the hand, join in; how the body is gently alive in the effort – and how this combined effort makes speaking so much easier. Here, if you wish, is a consolidation to your work of the greatest happiness.

Remember that the voice may vary with your mood or your physical condition. If you have a really important speech to make, strive, as near to it as possible, to relax for twenty to thirty minutes; lie down, or, at least, put up your feet.

This being the concluding chapter of the first part of the book, which has covered all the principles of speaking in public, it is appropriate to have a final word about the audience – our fellow men and women – of which we ourselves are so often members.

When all these principles are digested, they amount to one thing – good manners. The second commandment has so many wise applications to the practical situations of life. To be 'en rapport' with the audience is the key to speaking. From the beginning it has been insisted that an audience and the speaker are one, and that the object of any speech is the bringing of an idea, or a group of related ideas, and an audience together. Thirdly, it has been insisted that, a speech being merely a disciplined enlargement of a responsible conversation between two, the speaker must look at and traverse the audience almost the whole time. (The reaction of a nervous pupil wearing glasses just for reading, when advised he must get bi-focal or 'half-glasses', has been known to be – 'But I don't *want* to see the audience !'.) If a speaker fails to regard his audience continuously, his speech becomes a discourteous soliloquy.

A natural and experienced speaker will when the need arises conduct an audience rather like an orchestra. In an important political meeting or the last tired afternoon of a business conference, he will rouse individuals or knots of the audience like a conductor gaining response from, for instance, the second violins or the wind instruments. Essentially this is done pleasantly, akin to leg-pulling – so gaining the goodwill not just of the culprit but of all present (and gaining their future close attention).

Finally, remember that members of the audience may be nervous of *you* – it is not always the other way round. As you start and traverse them smoothly, you catch the eye of a man or woman, here and there, who at once drop their gaze. The next time, they hold it a little. The third time, as your eyes skim over the audience, they hold it entirely, friendliness in their eyes. You are pulling away the blanket, you are becoming 'en rapport' – your judges are beginning to approve your effort. Speak *to*, not at, people. A test that a speech has succeeded will be that members later say to you 'You know, we all felt that you were speaking to each of us individually'.

Part 2

9 The Microphone

Unless you must, do not use the microphone. At the beginning of this century, Members of Parliament, quite unaided, had to address audiences of 5,000 to 6,000 at election time. Its use has become too much a status symbol in small establishments catering for functions; too much an invariable habit in leading establishments which speakers worth their salt should quietly refuse. Most regrettably it has become a fixture in regular use in most churches, thus on the one hand encouraging the preacher not to use the full range of his voice; on the other hand often ignoring the unsuitability of such high echoing buildings. The use of a microphone cannot *improve* the personality of a speaker; it *can* cause loss of personality.

The microphone is your servant, not your master. Accordingly, speak *towards* it, not *into* it. Put in another way, do not look at the instrument as you are speaking. If you are inexperienced and nervous there is a desire, if you do look at it, to crane nearer and nearer. For a standing microphone, there has always to be some permissible angle of traverse and, within this angle, be sure to look over the audience as you should normally; do not let the instrument in any way freeze the natural expression of your face.

What can the microphone accomplish that is impossible for the human voice alone? There appear to be five advantages. First, where there is an overflow meeting, when many of the audience will only be able to hear the speaker. In such a case, it is a happy courtesy to walk the speaker through the unsighted rooms – in the most natural manner, as if he and the chairman were on their way to the main hall; or, informally but courteously, to pause a moment to introduce him. The second suggestion warms both him and the unsighted members – the blanket is being smoothly pulled away. (Even for short circuit television, this suggestion is worthy of consideration.)

Secondly, the microphone is without rival in the open air – from the Pope, speaking whilst overlooking the tens of thousands in St Peter's Square, to the vicar's wife opening the village fête – where she may have happily to compete with the wind in the trees, the children's voices and the distant sound of 'fair' music.

Thirdly, if hecklers at a public meeting abuse their power and just shout to disrupt, the chairman has every right to take advantage of his microphone and warn them firmly of the legal position. Be sure the meeting is on enclosed premises – be it a building or a sports field – for only in such circumstances do those abusing their right and properly warned lose their status as invitees and become trespassers liable to be removed. Using a microphone unnecessarily at such meetings will appear heavy-handed and unfair.

Fourthly, if a speaker wishes to speak in a relaxed, conversational manner to a large audience, he can remain seated for his speech and have the microphone moved in to about one foot in distance. In the great financial crisis in the world on the turn of the thirties, and even more effectively in the Second World War, President Roosevelt used to give 'fireside chats' on the radio to his countrymen, visualising a group of two or three people listening to him as they sat around the fire.

Applying this habit to a live audience, of even 1,000, speakers such as Churchill or Beaverbrook, invited out in their old age by countless acquaintances to celebrate a personal anniversary, could speak in a crisp conversational manner whilst seated. Similarly, speakers of any age convalescing from illness or accident may be able to keep faith with their hosts by remaining seated. (There is, of course, nothing to prevent such a seated speaker, if he wish, speaking in full voice – he simply keeps the instrument, suitably lowered, at standing distance.)

Finally, for answering questions after a speech, when you have a large audience, to sit down and adopt this crisp conversational tone is ideal. As said in chapter 12, it fits in with the more intimate atmosphere needed as the audience comes into its own.*

The technique of using the microphone depends mainly on two considerations – the proper tone of voice and the proper distance, of length, height and traverse (the 'necklace' and hand microphones each demand a separate note). As to tone, increase your power rather than heighten your pitch. As a rough guide, imagine that you are throwing the voice ten to fifteen yards away. But, as in speaking normally, you have the real solution in your control – as you begin, watch the reaction of those at the back. Are their faces strained or do they look a little deafened? However, when you are sitting down, the microphone drawn in closely, speak then as if a person was sitting at the other end of a table, six to eight feet away. In both cases, obey the advice given as to posture in chapter 6 – particularly keeping the feet still when standing, and not swaying the body about when sitting.

The trouble that arises when advice is offered about distances is that microphones vary so much in type, whether amongst contemporary models or, more particularly, through the passage of time. Leading London hotels and caterers, the the West End stage where appropriate, may insist on having always the latest model. But town halls and village halls; pleasant and efficiently run smaller hotels in the county towns, will not wish to be so professional.

As to length, one and a half to three feet is a good bracket. When you sit down for questions, have the instrument moved in to about one foot. Do not be influenced by the pop singer and the singer at the Palladium who almost suck the mouth-

* Given the circumstances, the microphone can claim another advantage. With a large audience, its volume lets you cover more ground – because you can speak faster than when you use the voice alone.

piece. If the roof of the theatre is not almost lifted off, the audience would expect their money back.

As to height, any position from just below the chin to the level of the breast should be suitable. The angle of the microphone – straight up or tilted – and the relation of your position to the audience will decide your exact choice. This selection will be mainly for best reception, but also so that you can be easily seen by the audience.

Finally, as to traverse, when speaking on your feet, 40° or more, each side, should be possible without the voice fading in the slightest. Clearly when you sit down and the microphone is placed nearer to you, the angle widens. (If you have a 'battery' of instruments, the angle is calculated from each flank.)

Regarding a microphone held in the hand, the tone of voice out of doors should be like that which you use when standing on the feet; and the tone of voice indoors should resemble that adopted when sitting down – as described above. Hold the instrument nine to twelve inches away, and just below mouth level (the position of the head when speaking normally has a slightly forward tilt). Keeping the elbow and part of the forearm against the side steadies the position. Without becoming stiff-necked, get your traverse more by turning the shoulders rather than by turning the head. When you use a hand microphone in the open air, be sure that no loudspeaker is directly in front of or directly behind your position (stand by the side of a car carrying a loudspeaker on its roof). Equally be sure not to speak towards a high wall that is close to you. In all these cases, you are almost certain to get a 'feedback' – which you personally will not be aware of.

Regarding a 'necklace' microphone, length has no application; nor has traverse – for you can turn through a full circle and the volume remains constant. Its harness is adjustable, and the instrument should hang nine to twelve inches below the chin. The 'necklace' is the one microphone whose meshed head is at a right angle to the sound of the voice. It is indeed sensitive. Do not fondle its lead whilst you are talking or preaching. In one well known London church adhesive tape has been put round the lead to prevent its scraping the stall when the vicar stands up to announce the hymn. The instrument may react by crackling if resting on a shirt front made of nylon. The tone of voice should be that of the 'fireside chat', of answering questions when sitting down. (Its installation in many churches has tragically taken away the clergy's power to speak vehemently on the right occasions. Not only a high quality of speaking but also a responsiveness not to be found in the average congregation are required to convey thoughts with effect when power has been removed from the full range of the voice.) The first advantage of the 'necklace' microphone has already been mentioned – its unlimited traverse. Secondly, it gives mobility to you – you can move from table to exhibit and still speak to the audience. Thirdly, the position of the instrument should make you hold or place your notes suitably high and keep your throat flexed correctly. Linked with the last point, the possible conflict when using a static microphone of obeying the rule to have notes about a yard away from the eyes whilst the lectern supporting the instrument is about one and a half feet away – is avoided (the conflict in this other instance is avoided by holding the cards).

The simple touch remains of having a quiet word beforehand with the hall or restaurant manager – do overcome any shyness. What an unnecessary tragedy it is, for you and the listeners, if, after you have prepared a speech carefully, you then do not 'marry it up' with the microphone that you use. Tell him what you propose doing, yet seek his advice – 'Good evening. I'm speaking here this evening. I usually stand (say) two feet away from the microphone, and I traverse about 40° – is that what you recommended here?' A good manager will be delighted that you have taken this interest. To be sure, the volume of sound can nearly always be adjusted 'behind the scenes' during a speech; but anyone taking pride in his efforts should aim to be right from the beginning. Naturally, you must stand still before the microphone – traversing gently as usual, save for remembering the arc that is permissible. You must not move in and out, or sway.

If the importance of the occasion makes you decide to call and see the layout, then you could raise this matter. If in addition you are offered a trial run for a minute or so, remember the sound of your voice will not be cushioned by the presence of an audience – and the comments of any friend listening must be used judiciously. (You do not hear your own voice amplified when you speak.)

If the manager, on either occasion suggested, is not responsive or even ignorant, then at your speech take charge yourself – as suggested earlier on when tone was discussed. Walk slowly in from one pace away, watching the reaction at the back. The right general tone can be struck either by varying the distance or by varying the voice. It does seem a pity that every standing microphone cannot bear a card, the size of a visiting card, carried in a slot suggesting the distance away the speaker should stand. But until every speaker realises the simple fact that where the eyes look the voice carries the suggestion cannot be fully effective.

Four small points remain. If you wish to make an emphatic point, as you do so take a short careful pace backwards (almost rock back). If you not do this, you risk there being a 'feedback'.

It is best for the microphone to be adjusted in height, even in distance, by the meeting's organiser or an official of the place. Too much handling by different hands, belonging to those rightly concentrating on their speaking, may cause a break in the connection at a crucial moment. If you do handle the instrument yourself, do so with consideration.

Thirdly, if you have to make a series of announcements from a car, as in the cavalry on reconnaissance before war became mechanised, do move by bounds. Stop the car and make the announcement at strategic points on the route. The thoughtless stupidity of an indistinct voice surging to a roar and fading away again has lost many votes at elections.

Finally, if an audience becomes accustomed to the invariable use of the microphone, they are apt to believe that they cannot hear without it! A good speaker should hold fast : and with courtesy and friendliness – even banter – explain the position.

10 Visual Aids

Visual aids – actual articles or models, charts or blackboard sketches, slides or films – should be used only if they improve the spoken word. They may be so much part of the address that without them it is meaningless. On the other hand, used without imagination they can spoil the rhythm of a talk and prevent a linked pattern forming in the listener's mind.

So far as necessary, keep them completely out of sight, or at least covered up, until they are required. In this way you retain the maximum concentration of the audience. For a speaker on foreign affairs, a map constantly in position may give the right atmosphere; and will probably be too detailed to distract the audience without his lead. For an architect, a model may be relevant from the beginning; on the other hand, if covered up until this relevant moment later appears it gives an air of expectation. Charts or blackboard sketches should either be covered up or turned round until reference to them is necessary.

Be sure that the lighting is of the best, and, if possible, view material sketched or written on a blackboard from various angles of the audience to guard against shine. The same caution is needed with charts mounted on a shiny surface.

Think out beforehand how best you can address the audience whilst referring to the chart or sketch. Do your utmost to look towards its members as often as possible, especially when you are speaking. This implies being sideways on both to exhibit and audience; and as near level with the former as possible. A pointer may be of assistance. A model will normally allow you to stand mainly behind it (be sure it is high enough to be clearly seen). The art is to gauge how much time initially to give an audience to take in the exhibit; how much time to pause between your remarks as you proceed. The simple test is to put yourself always in their place; their state of mind is like yours was when you first made up the chart, or when you started your sketch. Good judgement will retain their maximum concentration on your words. The same sensitive judgement applies when you hand out a document to each member of the audience; how far you give them time individually to browse, how far you guide them through it.

If the exhibit no longer has relevance and may distract the audience as you continue, then cover it up or remove it.

If you are one of many lecturers at a conference, clearly careful timing is essential. To time a speech by a rehearsal is always necessary; but here the problem is more difficult because of the breaking up of its rhythm when exhibits have to be dwelt on. Clear forethought in general is very important, for visual aids can belie their name and become a handicap unless the arrangements required are carefully anticipated. Until a lecture or demonstration is well established, a careful rehearsal and, where possible, a previous visit to the scene are most advisable.

If using a film, be sure to dovetail the speech most carefully with it. Unless you deliberately wish to endorse various points by both means, speech and film, some of the matter could become redundant. Time too may dictate to you which to cut.

The use of slides deserves particular mention, notably when used by the doctor and the scientist, where their value may be crucial, even vital – to emphasise what has been said or to illustrate in their own right. If the lecture hall or room is unknown to you, strive to check it beforehand. Can the lights, which must be completely out for colour slides and radiographs, be easily half-dimmed for print? If you have to refer to notes in the gloaming or the complete gloom, make sure the lighting necessary has no effect on the main exhibits.

Prior liaison with the projectionist is advisable to avoid

G

the slides going in the wrong way around, going in too soon, coming out too late; and to ensure correct focusing. Many slides, such as of pathological specimens, can be focused only by one knowledgeable in the subject, the usual technician being out of his depth. Such a knowledgeable person should sit by the projectionist to help when necessary. The ideal in such circumstances is the use of the automatic projector, which gives one-man control, with its long lead to the lecturer and its two-buttoned switch for changing and for focusing slides. To project the slides beforehand is important – at least it ensures they fit! Modern transparencies eliminate the risk of glass slides being dropped at crucial moments – though an overheated projector may redress the balance and melt them!

If words are to appear on a slide, then legibility is the first requirement. Again, do not overwhelm people with too much writing. Three to four short lines should suffice, which would require ten to fifteen seconds to digest. Do keep silent during this time, enlarging, if need be, thereafter. The capital letters of a good typewriter are a good medium for this writing, but good print is the best of all, for each letter is spaced according to its size.

Slides must be numbered, which is necessary also for reference if there is a question time. Also be sure to duplicate their numbers in your notes. If you are caught out by an unmarked slid being projected upside down, the way of correcting this is simple. Hold it so that the writing can be read and the subject is the right way up. Then rotate it 180° anticlockwise and place it in the carrier.

11 After-Dinner Speaking

Far too much fuss is made over this type of speech and, in result, the naturalness, which must be its essential characteristic, is apt to be lost. In season, the masters and prime wardens of more than eighty livery companies in the City of London endeavour to justify their spurs by pounding their way through numerous speeches. The lodges of freemasonry and kindred institutions reinforce this tradition. Countless firms, clubs and associations of all types have at least an annual dinner; whilst throughout the year, weddings and other celebrations demand their word.

Part of the trouble is that this may be the only type of occasion that a person speaks on his feet, and, understandably, he does not wish to make a fool of himself or let others down. The contrast between the happy nature of the occasion and his feelings towards the task seems to him severe. Yet the main trouble is the feeling, almost the tradition, that it is necessary to be amusing. This conjures up the need to drag in one or more jokes at any price; to try and turn oneself for the occasion into a leading comedian. In fact the key quality on these occasions is friendliness. Here it takes and retains the lead throughout the race from authority. You are speaking to the most amiably disposed audience of all, and therefore, a light-*hearted* contribution is called for. See that your manner matches your matter – be friendly in the only possible way, by remaining natural. 'Light-hearted' does not mean 'lightheaded'. (Refer to chapter 5, p 52, on 'friendliness'.)

The audience is amiably disposed for many reasons. At the most cynical, they may have paid to come, or duty may demand their presence – they have to hear the speech, and accordingly hope it will be endurable. If selected guests, they may have a feeling akin to an invited audience at a television show, who are prepared to laugh so soon as a comedian puts his unknown nose round the corner of the stage. Moving up the scale of human kindness in our survey, the ladies have gladly paid particular attention to their appearance, probably by so doing instilling some feeling of occasion into the often reluctant male. Then the combination of good wine and food, the tinkle of cups and spoons and the aroma of cigars tends to mellow everyone, save a melancholic regular. But most important of all there remains the sense of occasion and the meeting with friendly people.

Always have a hard core of facts. In keeping with friendliness superseding authority, *how* you speak may, on this unique occasion, be more important than *what* you say; but only a brilliant and experienced speaker can stretch this to the extreme. A core of facts gives you confidence, and gives some satisfaction at least to those listening.

Facts and thoughts are not always easily come by in after-dinner speeches. Steer between platitudes and straining for effect. If you want to compliment the officers on their achievements in arranging the function, if you wish to praise the food and wine, if you wish to comment on the beauty of the ladies – try to do so in a balanced simple fashion.

You must not shirk, if need be, asking others to help you assemble facts. The organiser of the function, your friends, the guests' friends and even their secretaries may have to be approached.

If the remarks of the proposers at a dinner, or even those of the one proposing and the one replying to a toast, are likely to 'clash', a certain amount of informal liaison beforehand may avoid this.

Incline to brevity. Many livery companies – guilds over eighty in number, who derive their name from the distinctive dress (livery) assumed by their members in the fourteenth century – have a convention that the Master speaks at their dinners for the most for eight minutes. Remember that the speech should have some happy interruptions – of laughter, of clapping, of restrained banging on the table, of 'hear! hear!', and of a pleasant short quip thrown at you. Allow for these breaks in timing the speech.

Your general pace will be as slow as you will ever speak – in contrast to that of debate which can rise to the fastest. To speak as if you are in an annual general meeting of a company is fatal. Remember the key phrase 'relaxed authority' applied to stance; let it pervade the whole person. Have in mind, perhaps, the Scarlet Pimpernel – outwardly languid, but his brain working with great speed when need be. A slow pace does not mean a lazy pace and you will, of course, change it in keeping with what you are saying. Sensitive pausing is particularly needed (made easy by the interruptions of applause and other sounds), and keeping the voice up at the end of remarks helps greatly on such mellowing occasions.

Always remember the greatest question of all, 'What is my object?' For example, in toasting the guests, do not compliment at length the officers of the association or comment too long on what other speakers have said – and suddenly realise you have around half a minute for the proper task.

Timing gives quality to a speech, when quite a reasonable amount of applause is likely. It is a question of framing the language to gather up the applause. If, for example, you are welcoming, commenting on or praising individual guests, strive to leave their names, their titles to the end so as to avoid two rounds of applause, which as the speech progresses becomes more half-hearted. ('Now we come to one who behind the scenes has been such a power, who has . . . . . , who has . . . – our friend the Bishop of . . .')

If you have a standing microphone, be sure you find out the permissible angle of traverse, in which alone your voice will be consistently heard. Do not turn and 'pouter pigeon' with the president as you greet the audience. Acknowledge him with a friendly bow from the shoulders and swing into the audience to speak – as suggested in chapters 2 and 6. When referring to anyone present who is outside the arc, look towards him before and after speaking (if need be, during a pause in the speech).

Certainly, humour – a joke or an anecdote – is in its natural place at dinners. But the speech must in no way be bent to it; it must slip readily into the context of the speech. Humour basically is spontaneous or nothing. When you tell a joke or an anecdote, relive the scene and the emotion. This is the only occasion in public speaking when you break the fundamental rule of looking consistently at the audience. Save for an occasional glance, look over their heads reflectively as you 'paint the picture' (now in general a cliché, but here such an appropriate expression). Your general pace changes, as may your tone. Your pausing is sure to be longer as you build up the incident. If you stimulate another speaking, show some contrast to your own voice, but be wary of imitating marked dialects or accents. There is no question of looking like a dying duck in a thunderstorm as you reflect; lose yourself in the story and look natural. Really relive the scene to yourself, and remember that to the audience it is fresh, and so its description must not be hurried. Be concise.

Yet the greatest aids to being light-hearted are a lilt in the voice (demanding automatically a friendly look in the eye), and a happy turn of phrase, especially when leg-pulling. The turn of phrase will be helped considerably by the way the voice strokes the words.

A quotation here and there, if short and apt and if properly spoken in a necessary contrasting tone, is a useful ally.

Provided it is trimmed down to a reasonable length, say three-quarters of a minute in a five minute speech, a contribution of a serious turn may be welcome – but it must still be spoken in a light-hearted manner. For example, until very recently, if toasting 'The Champions' at the dinner and dance which concludes the Wimbledon tennis fortnight, you might say, having paid your compliments to the various winners and keeping the same lilt in the voice – 'And now, Mr President, may I dwell, just for one minute, on a serious matter?' (Pause at fair length whilst the tinkle of glasses and the buzz of humanity cease, and the guests alert themselves.) 'I am wondering just how long this most happy of occasions will continue unless we soon determinedly face one grave issue . . . . . I refer to "Shamateurism" . . . .' And then you, in simple authority, give your points. Yet to plough along on social occasions, such as a company's dinner and dance, with serious matters, heavily delivered, shows complete lack of imagination and is quite inexcusable. There are occasions, such as the Prime Minister speaking at a banquet at the Guildhall, when a serious speech of length is expected. There are occasions, such as the eminent guest speaking at a dinner of a livery company, 'the Pilgrims' or other all-male assembly when the time allotted to the serious part of the speech can be longer. But the principle of a serious contribution being short and spoken light-heartedly otherwise is all-embracing.

Dinners of a professional body, of a trade association, of the senior executives of a company fall just within the scope of this chapter. The speeches are apt to lean to the serious, to be longer and may review the past year. Even so, a friendly tone still blends very well with responsible matters. Often the comparatively relaxed and reflective nature of such a dinner – perhaps on the evening after the annual general meeting – gives a speaker a chance, firmly but sensitively, to bring up briefly an issue over which he has striven in vain at council or board meetings. Assuming he is a person well liked by his colleagues, the atmosphere may make all the difference. As they stroll away afterwards, they may well reflect there was something after all in what he had been striving for. Such an opinion would best be quietly and briefly put.

As to notes, for after-dinner speeches, half-cards come right into their own. One or several does not matter. Either hold them in the palm of the hand and remember to use the arm as a mobile lectern to raise the notes upwards and forwards; or improvise a rest for them. As a rest, waylay a couple of cigar boxes and on them stand your bubble brandy glass, or preferably, your port glass. Squeezing the cards to ensure they are not too springy, slip their bottom in the rim of the glass. The port glass particularly makes the cards stand very upright. With a little practice, the cards can quite easily be removed. Take a step forward, looking down at the cards; slip the top one up and out firmly and, as you step back, look up again at the audience. You may even write the notes so that this movement comes at a natural pause. Be sure the light is the best obtainable (and allowing for this not being perfect, incline to write or type the notes on the large side).

Even if you have the most relaxed of dinners, where you are on terms of Christian names with most present and feel a note quite unnecessary, to slip a visiting card bearing, say, the four key heads of your speech into the waistcoat pocket may not be too security-minded. If becoming rather too relaxed you 'drop a clanger' at which everyone roars with laughter – yourself above all, for the joke is on you – you may forget what you are saying.

All speaking in public to the sensitive speaker amounts, from one aspect, simply to being well mannered – bringing his facts and thoughts to the audience in the most agreeable way. This aspect applies particularly to after-dinner speeches when individuals are being mentioned. The art of praising and of thanking without laying it on with a trowel; the art of gentle leg-pulling, even of strangers; depend so much on the character and the good taste of the speaker. A good general rule to adopt is to place yourself in the recipient's place – would the thought or the way of expressing it jar or embarrass, or would its naturalness and sensitivity please?

A particular point may be made about the toast of 'The Guests'. If you are proposing this toast almost for certain you will name a few of them individually. This may ruffle the feathers of some others (or of their wives) who feel that they should have been mentioned. Bring in the editorial 'we' to mitigate this. For example, 'It will be obvious to all here tonight that, with the best will in the world, I cannot refer to all our guests individually; but I am sure that they would like me to mention particularly six of their number . . .'

Be sure to finish the speech well – in keeping with the universal rule. If you are proposing a toast, as you come to such climax show a little more authority in your carriage, and in the crispness and the power of the voice. There is no need to beseech the company 'to be upstanding', even 'to rise'. Keep the language simple : 'The toast is . . .' – 'I give you the toast of . . .' – 'Therefore with pleasure, I propose the toast of . . .' If you are replying to a toast, the authority may not be so marked, but you must still round off the speech efficiently.

Do not take your first words, your 'salutation' too much for granted; do not say it almost apologetically. A crisp, happy 'Mr President, . . . Ladies and Gentlemen', sets the tone to hold the audience. If you have a whole string of titles to reel off, certainly do not buffoon it, but try doing it with laughter, or at least light-heartedness, in the voice (implying that it is rather a bore, but you all appreciate that it has to be done). If you have any doubt about the correct title of address in the 'salutation' or in referring to an individual in the body of the speech, ring up firmly but with friendliness his secretary. Such approach will almost invariably be appreciated. Never let etiquette, for lack of such approach, spoil your peace of mind and take it away from the main task of speaking naturally.

If ever actually at a function you are asked to speak without warning – it does occur at times even in the best of circles – and you are at a loss, stay close to the audience. Speak about them, the occasion, and comment on what previous speakers have said. Without being disappointed, you should understand that no one can speak well extemporaneously unless he has a certain zest for life. Strive even at such challenges for a simple framework for your speech.

If speaking after others in general or replying to a toast in particular, you may, in a small way, have to add to or alter your speech. Do not, therefore crowd the cards. It may be useful to add any remark or note any change in a different coloured ink.

Luncheons and weddings deserve mention. Luncheons are

more varied in type than dinners. The business angle is often more prominent and speeches are expected to deal largely with serious and specialised issues. Toasting may not be part of the proceedings. Many lunches are specifically held to hear the opinions at fair length of a guest. Yet through all the varieties of lunchtime speaking, the speaker is wise to keep light-hearted and friendly in manner. Many deep shafts, as counsel and the good politician can testify, are often sunk whilst the manner remains light-hearted. After all the speech is hinged on food and drink – and Churchill and Bismarck have both paid serious tribute to the aroma of the cigar. Yet there is a sharper cutting edge to a lunch address. The audience have not entirely sloughed off their executive mood, and the day's work has not ended. Therefore do not be so relaxed as at dinner; do not be so mellow in pace. Be particularly careful about time. Goodwill which you have steadily built up can be easily lost if the time allotted is exceeded through the chairman's over-generosity; for many have appointments to keep.

Speeches at weddings can be tricky. Those listening are certainly amiably disposed, but the champagne has begun to work; the discipline and emotions of the church service are fading. Yet for the bride and, if he be wise, the bridegroom also, this is the greatest day of their lives. The parents for their part, particularly the mothers, realise it marks the end of a chapter.

Wedding receptions almost invariably these days have a running buffet. This makes the speaker's task more difficult, for informality is complete. Be sure you hoist yourself a little above the throng. If there is no platform and the caterers have not the imagination to supply a small dais, stand on a chair – perhaps with a kind friend unobtrusively holding it with his weight. Without being other than friendly, refuse to start speaking until everyone is quiet – the toastmaster, the father and many of the guests will hush down the 'rebels'. This prominence of position and demand for quietness are a courtesy due to the bride and bridegroom – not to puff up your own importance. Not the slightest sign of being solemn must appear. But you can still say sensitively chosen and serious things in a light-hearted manner, to blend with any foolish things you wish to say. This pattern applies also to the bridegroom and any other speakers.

Do not be frightened of the uniforms, of the dress of ceremony prominent at so many dinners. Uniform is necessary on many occasions in life to give authority, to bolster personalities and it can help many women; but it has no right to influence the light-hearted yet responsible contribution of an after-dinner speaker. Again, the repeated crashing of a gavel, wielded by a crimson-jacketed toastmaster, can rival the trump of doom to an inexperienced speaker. The solution is, a few times before your speech, to crash a tablespoon on some harmless wooden surface at home.

12 Answering Questions

One of the principles of war is immediate consolidation after attack. One of the first things drummed into a sprinter is to run right through the tape. This advice is equally essential for the speaker both as regards the conclusion of his address and this appendix of question time. Indifferently handled, the latter can mar a good speech; well handled, it can pull up a mediocre one (it is the audience's last impression of the speaker).

The strategy depends on two principles, the tactics number around ten.

As to the strategy, first, the atmosphere should become an 'editorial we' atmosphere. Here is where the members of the audience come into their own. In spirit, you descend into the arena to join them. With the chairman's agreement, take the questions sitting down. Relax, yet keep alert in mind and disciplined in posture – do not slummock about, but sit as suggested in chapter 6. Unless you are a guest speaker at a lunch or dinner of a relaxed nature do not smoke. It is always advisable – even in lunch hour meetings – for the chairman to arrange a two or three minute break after the speech so that the speaker can get his second wind and, equally important, so that the audience can wriggle and talk quietly to each other. If the audience is large and there is a microphone, have the latter placed nearer to you – about one foot away – and adjusted to your height so that you can speak in a crisp conversational tone. (Chapter 9 describes the simple technique of using the microphone.) Of the three main qualities a speaker should have, sincerity is here at a premium.

Some speakers, in keeping with the subject and the quality

of the audience, like to hear three or four questions then stand up to give the answers. This is a pleasant alternative and if you wish to use it yet speak in a more relaxed way, remember to have the microphone, although unaltered from speaking height, moved in to a foot's distance.

The second principle of strategy is to *keep to the point*. Be short, but not abrupt in your answers. The object is for as many people as reasonably possible to ask relevant questions. So many speakers, in their conceit or lack of common sense, break into minor speeches, so destroying the whole intention of this period.

The first of the tactics is to be friendly – as the term is used in this book. Always be firm, yet on this base, completely fair. Never be aggressive or personal, even if a question be delivered well below the belt (and the chairman sees fit not to interfere. In such a case, drop your head for a few seconds, keeping otherwise quite still – to keep your composure and mark your disapproval. Then look at the questioner, more fixedly than usual, probably without traversing the audience at all, and answer quietly but firmly. The sympathy you will gain will be considerable. Yet had you flared up, although the audience would have understood, they would have been sorry. An audience takes to itself a remark made to one of its members.

If a short reply is not possible, make the main points and promise to send fuller details by post, through the organisation running the meeting (in case the reply interests others as well). If circumstances permit, an alternative may be to suggest the questioner comes to you after the meeting is over.

Unless the answer is very simple, always think before you reply. Look over the audience's head or drop your gaze whilst reflecting; then come out with the answer. Time is not wasted for the answer should be clear-cut and the members of the audience will have been thinking what they would say themselves.

Do not look fixedly at the questioner when you reply. Glance at him in the beginning and at the end, perhaps in between;

but, with good manners, traverse all the audience, making them share the problem.

Within the bounds of time, be sure a questioner is satisfied (otherwise, circumstances permitting, suggest he sees you after the meeting has closed). This, if done sincerely, builds up general goodwill.

Pay tribute to a good question – good in its own right or helping what you have said. This comes best if done so soon as the question is posed; but if tribute has been paid twice or more already, vary the gesture by thanking the member after you have answered.

If a question needs repeating, because it is inaudible, because it is badly put, because it is a 'portmanteau' question (there is also an art in *asking* questions), it is best, by pre-arrangement, for the speaker to do this. If the chairman does it, a third voice breaks in unnecessarily. More particularly, in the case of a badly put question, and a lengthy question that has to be both 'translated' and shortened, the speaker is the person to do this. He has to answer them – and the questioner will soon pull him up if he has misinterpreted the point.

If you do not know the answer, normally make no attempt to bluff. Admit happily but not irresponsibly such a position – 'I am afraid you have knocked me out right away!' After a pause, add 'Can anyone help us?' Whatever happens, you have shown your sincerity. If no one can, make clear you will find out, and pass the information to the organisation concerned by note. Do not forget to thank the questioner (and anyone who has helped you). Clearly you would not wish this to happen with the first question, but if you have spoken well and know your subject, still take it lightheartedly – 'Well, there is nothing like being stymied by the first question! But I have to admit . . .'

If you do not but *should* know the answer – particularly if you are wearing two hats – take a happy chance and throw the question back to the audience. This tactic assumes that you have answered with success already a number of questions. Do it with panache – 'That is an excellent question . . .

Would anyone like to have a shot at it?' Almost for certain someone here, someone there will rise to the bait, especially if encouraged by you – 'Yes, I think that helps us quite a lot, sir. Would anyone else like to put in a word?' Then smilingly you sum up – 'I think, madam, that sets you well on the way to an answer'. But if you get no help at all, and everyone switches their eyes to you as the oracle, after a long pause, emulate the Mad Hatter in *Alice in Wonderland,* and shrugging the shoulders and smiling broadly, say 'I have not the slightest idea!' Then, when the laughter has died down, swiftly add 'But I will at once find out and advise you. And thank you, sir, for opening up such new points of interest and teaching us all what gaps we have to fill.'

Business men of high repute but inexperienced as speakers often find themselves at ease when they are answering questions. There are lessons to be drawn from this. How foolish, each might reflect, that when speaking he had not realised the audience were the pleasant and keen people he later found them to be. How easily too the facts and thoughts flowed at question time; he had no fear at all about his language. How naturally also he was able to look at people. How interesting he found it all, quite losing himself in the subject. The next time he speaks . . . !

Some subjects lend themselves more to questions and answers than others; or, the members of the audience may be as knowledgeable, as intelligent as the speaker. In such circumstances, the speech may be little more than an anchor for a session of questions. If you are not of high repute, it is wise before the occasion to discuss such an approach with the organisers. But unless you *are* talking to a knowledgeable audience, a certain foundation must be laid by you in a speech, otherwise, no matter how interested the audience shows itself to be in the questions, the object in presenting the subject in some symmetry will be defeated.

Heckling, in its strict meaning applicable only to political meetings, is dealt with below. But often at meetings in general is the person who is rather full of himself, and over-enthusiastic in asking questions. It is, of course, the chairman's duty to suggest, to order, that he give way until others too have had their say. But if the chairman is weak, then either you must make such a point through him, or, firmly but pleasantly yourself ask the questioner to stand down until others as well have ventured.

For those interested in politics, a word about varying your style of answer, and about heckling may be useful. Political audiences vary greatly, but normally there will be three elements – the agreeing, the doubtful and the disagreeing, the first and third showing little resilience of view. For the first, appeal to reason. For the second, stress what common ground there may be between you, then, bit by bit, try and take them away – 'I have never heard it expressed like that before . . . . , but . . .' For the last element, at least try and make them appreciate your effort; concede a point here and there, then follow with 'But . . .' The patience shown over the third group could have a good impression on the important middle group.

Heckling means to tease with questions. The sole object of a heckler is to take you out of your stride. Be determined from the beginning to be patient and merry about his efforts, and almost invariably ignore his questions or remarks. If he gives you an opening for a short crushing answer, then do step in speedily, be your reply a humorous riposte or a straight answer. Never be personal to a heckler, for a political audience can be easily incensed. If the question is shrewd and relevant, indicate you will be dealing with the point in a moment. If heckling gets out of control, as so often sadly happens these days, it is the chairman's responsibility to act. If he is a little hesitant, look towards him meaningfully, or, just ask if he intends to take any action. Do not be baited by the silent heckler – pretending to be asleep, regularly yawning, reading a newspaper which he opens out loudly. A smile in his direction at times gains you the audience's favour.

13 Debate

Debate should give rise to the highest form of speech. A lecture is informative. A speech, in all its range, may also be persuasive, especially when made as an appeal. But speeches in debate *must* be persuasive. The sole object is to induce those present to vote for your views. Consequently, your arguments must be well marshalled, and based on equally well chosen facts. It may be, if you present them well, the facts will speak for themselves. The attack must still be mainly made on members' minds, but an appeal to their sentiments, if you do it sensitively, is important. Such an appeal must never lead to haranguing – the young cousin to 'rabble rousing'.

Real formal debate occurs daily only in the meetings of legislative assemblies and the councils of local authorities. Unhappily, in the House of Commons, the stress of modern life does not encourage debate of the quality common at the beginning of this century (fortunately, in the more relaxed atmosphere of the Lords debates of high standing can, from time to time, be heard). Nor does the scope of local authorities' work normally give rise to debates throbbing with adventure or romance. Moreover, because of the important nature of the decisions dependent on such debates, and the diverse views of the parties involved, procedure governing them is apt to be complicated. Skilled use of it can be an art in itself, at times sadly looming larger than the substance of the debate.

Yet in everyday life there are several counterparts of such bodies, where the need of sincere factual persuasion is pre-eminent, and where, fortunately, the rigid procedural machinery that can threaten debate is absent – the council meetings of national bodies, of trade associations and trade unions; the board meetings of limited companies and corporations; and committee meetings of all sizes and importance held regularly throughout the land. Apart, therefore, from the practice of debate giving a finer edge to your individual speeches, here lies the importance of the studying of some of its principles.

A speech in a debate has two outstanding features, the first of which has already been mentioned – that it is persuasive or nothing. The second is that it is a blend of careful preparation and spontaneity. How well this second characteristic equips you for committee work. For any meeting of substance you study the agenda beforehand and make notes affecting the headings on which you must be ready to speak. Then at the meeting a colleague drastically cuts across some of your views, which demands a reappraisal of what you were going to say. Matters also may be raised on other points on the agenda which affect you. Almost spontaneously you may have to express an opinion. The quality of lucid thought before the mouth is opened, which is gained by the practice of preparing speeches, and the experience of crossing swords in debate – for a debate is essentially a duel – will stand you in good stead.

The merits of debating societies are discussed in Appendix B. Well run societies will always have a worthwhile part to play, particularly if they keep three matters in mind. First, a number of members take delight in the technicalities of procedure – more in the business preceding the debate proper. If this gets out of hand it becomes childish and puts off the friendly but mature member. Secondly, it is essential that the main speakers master their subject. Others attending will be a mixture of those who have prepared something in fair detail, those who have brooded over the subject from time to time and those, deliberately or not, who have come along quite unprepared. Unless the subject is securely anchored in the beginning, the debate can become an empty waffle. This point is often aggravated by the third – that so many of the subjects chosen are lacking in sinew, the titles often being merely a way of showing a committee's or secretary's clever-ness. No debating society can possibly be successful if its main speakers are unwilling to prepare their speeches with care. There is no need to be solemn; a responsible debate can be full of all the pleasant qualities.

Always be sensitive to good manners in a debate. When you provoke your opponent by the direct attack of your speech, or when you cross swords with him by criticising what he has said, never be rude, nor, preferably, sarcastic. Be careful to ridicule not your opponent but his case. Do not, for example, say 'Mr President, never before have I heard such a ridicu-lous member argue a case'; but 'Mr President, never before have I heard such a ridiculous argument'.

There is, of course, ample scope for humour – when you are experienced and know how to relax yet remain in com-mand of yourself. But the same advice stands as for general speaking; bend the humour to the speech, not the speech to the humour. Take care not to make the humour so success-ful that it distracts from your main object. Friendliness throughout is a good lubricant to your authority.

On the proposer lies the onus of proving the case. Let him exploit this advantage to the full, choosing the most favour-able battleground. The opposer clearly has two tasks – posi-tively to establish his own case and secondly to destroy his predecessor's. It follows his own prepared speech will not take up all the time allotted to him.

How and when should a speaker attack his opponent's speech? Particularly when you are not fully experienced, it is wise not to launch all your shafts so soon as you stand up. Your impromptu speaking will not be of the quality of your prepared speech, and to throw in everything right away will mean that the important first impression made on the House may be mediocre, hesitant or scratchy. Even when you are experienced, it is good tactics to fire just a broadside or so at first, leaving other points of disagreement to be demolished when they come up during your own positive argument.

Each of the leading speakers has a supporting speaker.

Their task, with less time available, follows the pattern of the opposer's. The third speaker will add to and endorse his leader's case and comment on that of the opposer. The fourth speaker will add to and endorse his leader's case and comment on that of his predecessor (and that of the proposer, if need be). The leaders will have liaised with their second strings and have given them a side of the case to argue complementary to their own main attack. This should not exclude their ability to endorse the major points of their respective leader's case, which done in their own personal language, can impress a point on members more strongly.

If a certain body of fact, common to both sides, needs revealing to lay a foundation for the debate, then the proposer should undertake this task – and the opposer should acknowledge his courtesy in so doing. For example, if there is a motion that capital punishment should be restored in Great Britain, the proposer in his opening remarks should lucidly remind the House of the previous legal position.

When the four leading speakers have performed, the debate is thrown open to the House. There is no need as you conclude your own speech to declare allegiance to either side. In integrity, you should not; for a succeeding speaker of ability may make you change your views. Hence the habit of many presidents alternately saying 'Would any member wish to speak for the motion?' then, 'Would any member wish to speak against the motion?' should not be followed. All is well if the phrases are not used as a chant, but only occasionally are spoken individually to stimulate lagging support for one side.

When no one else wishes to speak from the floor of the House – or through the passing of time the president has to rule no more contributions are possible – the proposer exercises his right of reply. So far, he has been the only speaker who has had no chance to counter-attack. He can now cope with *all* opponents and also endorse his own major arguments. He is not allowed to raise any *new* matter. The time permitted is about a quarter of the length of the main speech.

Sometimes the opposer as well is given a right of reply. In which case he will precede the proposer (and possibly will not be allotted so long).

How do you prepare for debate, as one of the leading speakers? In principle, as you do for any other type of worthwhile speech (as suggested in chapter 2). Well ahead of the day, sit down and reflect on the task, jotting down any facts and ideas that come to you. Add to these in the next few days – by further reflection, by picking up points from your newspaper, by questioning friends and colleagues over lunch or over a drink in the evening. Still comfortably ahead of the day, work out, if possible, your main points and arguments. Finally, comes research.

In debate, the president, in fairness to each side, must have no mercy as to time. Keep this well in mind as the material starts to pile up.

Such a speech must have no puppy fat; it must be one of bone and sinew. Always keep the motion well in mind. Your facts and thoughts, in such persuasive speaking, must all be pegged to it. On the other hand, thin arguments down to the main issues, so that you can the more effectively hammer them into the audience's head.

Yet in this type of speaking there is one more step you can take. Emulate counsel preparing his case and put yourself in your opponent's place. List out the main arguments favouring each side. This should be considered from the beginning of your preparation. Thus you may strengthen your main points. If you are leading your opponent, you may be able to anticipate what he may say in your own remarks, and at least draw some of his sting. If you are following your opponent, you can now start sharpening your sword for 'cross-examination' of his speech.

Always keep alert before you speak, whether from the table or the floor, so that you may add to or modify your present arguments. Particularly must this apply when you are the opposer and, to a lesser degree, when you are speaking third or fourth. Apart from having a few spare cards to hand so that you may record completely fresh material, leave a fair margin in your notes for such comment (it may be in a different coloured ink). Alternatively, leave deeper spaces between your notes.

Equally, when you are the proposer you must in no way sag after your attack. Right away listen carefully to your main opponent, and then to the words of *all* the speakers to come. Thus, in your final right of reply you should be able to redress the balance by stressing your own major original arguments and by mitigating any reasoning hostile to your cause. The right of reply is of the greatest importance. The debate has ranged over a wide field. Here is the moment to draw up the reins. Let your tone, although remaining friendly, be incisive, for the audience may be a little weary. Remember how important it is in an ordinary speech to leave a good impression with the listeners. If you stammer out a few disjointed points at this stage, counting on the goodwill earned long ago in your opening speech, you will perhaps undo all the good then accomplished. The art in this final speech must be to sift during the course of the debate the considerable material you may amass as speaker follows speaker. It may be good tactics either to mark up the major points you propose endorsing on your original cards, or, before the occasion, list them on a separate card to be used in such right of reply. As the time of closure draws near, or you calculate there are only one or so potential speakers left, tick those points of the many you have amassed which seem most important – given the skill and time, perhaps numbering them. There is no need for your final speech to be a polished one; the hesitation of comment from time to time may be, in its naturalness, an advantage. But the speech must flow on the whole with vigour.

If you are speaking from the floor of the House, you may have come fully prepared, with a water-tight speech; just having given some quiet thought to the subject over the last few days; or quite unprepared. In each instance, keep alert from the beginning. You can gain experience from the debate

in each case. The fact that previous speakers cover the points
you had in mind does not mean you make no contribution.
In your own language you warmly endorse what others have
said, so playing a valuable roll in knocking a point more
firmly into members' heads.

This being the highest form of speech, all the major principles must be observed : cards clearly written and well spaced,
for you to consult with ease; cards rested and propped up on
some form of support so that your eyes, the cards and the
eyes of the audience furthest away are roughly in line. If you
prefer to, hold the cards – as the speakers from the floor will
have to – half-postcard in size, nestling in the palm of the
hand, and *raise* them upward and forward, when needed.

The simple sequence of debate can be easily described. Any
body meeting regularly must have some administration to
discharge, if it is at times only recording its last meetings,
before the debate itself starts. The President is flanked on his
right by the Treasurer, the Proposer and the third speaker;
on his left by the Secretary, the Opposer and the fourth
speaker.

1. 'Order! Order! I call on the Secretary to read the minutes of
   the last meeting.' (Secretary stands up and reads.)
2. 'Is it the wish of the House that I sign these minutes as a
   correct record?' (If 'Aye', move to '4'; if 'No', move to '3'.)
3. 'Does any honourable member wish to question the accuracy
   of these minutes?' (Discussion follows resulting in agreement.)
4. 'Is there any question arising out of the minutes?'
5. 'Is there any matter of private business?'
6. 'There being no (further) private business, the House will proceed to public business. The motion before the House tonight
   is:
       '. . . . .'
   It will be proposed by Mr . . . and opposed by Mr . . . Mr . . .
   will speak third and Mr . . . will speak fourth. I call on
   Mr . . . to propose the motion.'

Notice the distinction between points 3, 4 and 5.

The courtesies of debate can be reduced to four. First,
speakers address the chair in the style 'Mr President, Sir', or

'Mr President', or just 'Sir'. It is best to use the full phrase in the beginning. You do not address, as you do in normal speaking, anyone else ('Mr Chairman, Ladies and Gentlemen'). During your speech, keep the President alert from time to time by one of these refrains and bring the members in by referring to 'the House' or 'Honourable Members'. By convention, the last two are never used as direct greetings, as a 'salutation', or bracketed directly with the President. They slip in more naturally – 'I would ask the House . . .' – 'Honourable members will give full weight . . .' If a lady is president, then she will be addressed as 'Madam President' or 'Ma'am' – the first always being used in starting a speech.

Secondly, only the President addresses members by name, and then usually only when calling on them to speak. Members are referred to as 'the honourable member who spoke last', 'the honourable member on my right', 'the Honourable Proposer', 'the Honourable Secretary' and suchlike. There are no ladies and gentlemen in debate.

Thirdly, there are occasions when a member wishes to challenge what a speaker is saying. Two of these challenges should become familiar to you – 'On a point of explanation . . .' and 'On a point of order . . .' The first is normally peculiar to a previous speaker whose figures have been wrongly quoted, or whose meaning has been deeply misunderstood ('On a point of explanation, Mr President, I did not say "30,000" children – I said "13,000" '). The second involves a graver issue and is open to anyone. A common example would be if the proposer in his right of reply tried to introduce new matter – and the President had failed to act himself ('On a point of order, Mr President, the Honourable Proposer is introducing material in no way mentioned before in the House this evening'). The member wishing to challenge should stand up smartly and preface his query with the appropriate challenge. The President then considers if the correction is necessary, the other party having meanwhile given way and sat down.

Fourthly, if the President wishes to speak in the debate, he asks either the Treasurer or the Secretary to take the chair –

the chair then being addressed as 'Mr Chairman'. (This is not
a habit to be encouraged. Its only justification is when a debate
is running lamely. Then a sensitive – not a forcible – contribution by the President, preferably giving facts and thoughts
some of which favour the motion, some of which go against
it, can bring back life to the meeting.)

The ability to speak spontaneously and extempore deserves
the final word. In neither case has this anything to do with
the 'gift of the gab' or the ability to talk about nothing.
Spontaneous speaking of quality implies a man has fairly
deep knowledge of his subject, is intelligent and is quick in
the uptake. It does not prohibit a slight pause before speaking – for example, in replying to a question. Because it is an
involuntary desire, an impulse, it may in its naturalness be
of great effect. Extempore speaking, a wider term, may lack
spontaneous desire, but the three qualities just mentioned as
necessary for good spontaneous speaking are an asset.

The ability to speak with no real preparation is invaluable
in all the circumstances of general life. It may be at its most
skilled in public speaking, but it is invaluable also in the
answering of questions after a speech, in the cut and thrust
of committee work, in business negotiations and in interviews
of all kinds.

Apart from the general discipline of speaking, as described in
this book, having its gradual effect on such skill, is there any
particular way of helping its development? Debating societies,
from time to time, have what is called a 'hat debate'. Slips of
paper, bearing the title of simple subjects, are put in a hat
and members in turn have a dip and try and speak on their
subject for a prearranged short time. In talking about debating societies in Appendix B, we deride as a main achievement the ability to stand up and talk about nothing. But there
is no doubt that in its proper place and for its proper purpose a 'hat debate' is admirable – to sharpen the brain, to
give confidence and to allow of sincere humour and friendliness leading to relaxation. A pleasant adaptation of such a
debate is for three to five (not too many) friends to meet around

the fire for this purpose. The practice must be responsible –
'serious' as the term has been used in this book – but on such
a foundation much happiness can be had. To start, with, at
least, keep the subjects simple and the time short – one
minute may suffice. A one-word subject may do; for instance
– 'hats', 'beards', 'spectacles', 'shoes'; 'bus', 'hovercraft',
'ship', 'train', 'plane'. Mix the subjects. Too complicated a
subject to start with may cause hesitation, long-winded statement, or 'ers'. Part of the value of this exercise is to acquire
the habit of speaking in short but not abrupt sentences, and in
simple language. Stand up properly to speak, as if addressing
an audience of fair size. Each speech must be thoroughly criti-
cised, either by one member particularly detailed, or by each
in turn.

14 Open-Air Meetings

This is a unique form of public speaking, which is of interest mainly to the politician, and it is from his angle that this chapter is written. Certainly television has lessened the impact of such meetings; but at least when elections approach, they have their importance.

As in all speaking in public, be sure of your object. Broadly, it is to arouse and retain interest in your party. You are showing the flag, you are taking politics to the people. But particularly at election time, be alert also to feel the pulse of the electorate. Views may be thrown up by them, for example on race relations, on housing, from an angle not previously considered.

The strategy is dictated by one factor – the audience is always partly shifting. What are the tactics? First, size up each audience according to your general experience of the neighbourhood, for as a rule it is the voting residents you will be interested in. Size up each audience as well according to the actual occasion – get the 'feel' of the crowd, bearing in mind the time of day (the lunch hour, the evening, Saturday morning). Has the news of the day raised any topical issues?

Put your speech across at all costs. Accordingly, it is best to have just two or three points and let them develop. Be sure you are crystal clear, simple in words and in exposition. Hammer the points home, but not, of course, by sheer repetition of phrase. As to your facts, be right up to date. Talk of affairs of the moment, possibly the future – but be most careful about making promises. Avoid matters that may be easily misunderstood. Never waste time generally abusing the other parties; let your criticism of them be constructive.

Always be responsible in what you say, for nowadays there are many sensitive subjects.

It is a good opening to ask a question – which you will answer. Sometimes make up the speech entirely of questions, encouraging the audience to answer them (being sure that you are able, if need be, to answer them yourself). This string of queries can bring early life to a meeting; perhaps drawing the sting of hecklers or blending their teasing with some constructive 'give and take'.

At election time, when battle is officially joined, there is much to be said for basing the speech on points taken from election addresses. Whether you refer first to the other parties' or lead in with your own must be a matter of personal judgement.

Never stand idle on a platform (and be careful not to lean too much). It may at times be a good tactic to start chatting to one or two people on the ground, then gradually, to get up on the platform. Keep alive the whole time and remember how you gain authority. In the circumstances, to be a little larger than life is forgivable – gestures, for instance, need not be so restrained. Courtesy is important, and friendliness and a sense of humour vital. It is quite unforgivable and fatal to lose your temper – but an occasional well chosen outburst of mere annoyance can be very effective. Heckling is inevitable – and can be great fun.

As to the question, if long-winded, summarise them for all to hear. If the questioner is standing very close to you, try as an alternative, relaying his argument bit by bit to the crowd.

If you are using a microphone, be sure that you are at home with it. Test it at the opening of each meeting. A meeting can be ruined, and more lasting damage done to a party's standing, if you are coming across badly. Be very careful in the excitement of the moment never to harangue.

In this unique form of speaking you have to gather your own audience. To have two or three colleagues unobtrusively to help you is most valuable. One may be an experienced speaker. Then if someone defeats you with a question, you can cheerfully say 'The next speaker is going to tackle that subject'. Another may gently and skilfully shepherd the crowd. A third, making sure he is not distracting attention from the speaker at crucial times, may hand round literature – and even be able to enrol new members. A colleague as a heckler can be of help, particularly to gather the crowd and warm things up. Most of the listeners will not in the least mind discovering that he is on your side. Let the situation reveal itself, but then make a joke of it when things have warmed up a little – 'I didn't tell you to ask questions as difficult as that!'

The police must, of course, be told that you propose holding a meeting, and the site must be chosen in relation to traffic. A regular meeting at a regular place may well give you a valuable nucleus of supporters. Remember that a crowd begets a crowd.

A final tactic – remember to speak downwind, and if there is any discomfort from the sun, you should suffer it.

(Chapter 12, 'Answering Questions', is relevant to the holding of open-air meetings.)

15 Chairmanship

In this chapter there is nothing technical about motions and amendments, or about procedure that the law imposes on limited companies when their members or board meet. There are certain simple principles applicable to the chairmanship of all types of meetings, and a competent professional or business man when he is removed from the 'drill' of his smooth running committees to chair a meeting in public or to head an 'ad hoc' deliberative body may need reminding of them.

It is an advantage for a chairman to be an experienced speaker. This puts him 'en rapport' with both the speaker and the audience, giving him the sensitivity of being able to read an audience's mood and to help a speaker whenever this seems necessary. His ability may not be apparent save to the experienced; for the basic test of good chairmanship is that all goes smoothly. A first-class goalkeeper makes many shots easy to deal with by his anticipation in positioning himself, a quality most of the spectators may not appreciate.

What qualities should a good chairman have? First, you must exercise control – without appearing to dominate. This will be apparent in your judgement when to show authority – firmly and, ideally, quietly; how far to protect the speaker against interruption; how you rule in matters of dispute. You are the host, particularly to the speaker, generally to the audience. You are the liaison officer between them.

Secondly, you must show dignity without being pompous. This is a quality badly in need of restoration to life in general, and at all levels – the natural quiet dignity of the individual man and woman.

Thirdly, a sense of humour is an unrivalled asset. How often has the Speaker of the House of Commons, by a shrewdly timed and short intervention acted as a catalyst to the members approaching white heat? No other quality can help you to retain a sense of balance so well as this. It gives you the judgement when and how to intervene; to read the mood of the audience and restore proportion to the meeting by what you say and how you say it; and to ease in nervous speakers without taking away their dignity. Such friendly humorous touches must, however, always be subordinate to authority.

Fourthly, you need to have complete control of your temper. Even anger (which implies control of temper) is best concealed by calm authority. If you do lose your temper you have little option but to hand over the chair to another and retire; or, if you are big enough in spirit, to apologise and ask whether the meeting would like you to continue or to stand down.

Fifthly, as already hinted at, you should be a competent speaker. The tone of a meeting can be set by your opening remarks – by what you say and how you say it. It is true an experienced speaker will not be perturbed, he will just be sorry, if you are anaemic or clumsy; but the audience will not be pleased. Moreover, it is in your opening remarks that you can help a nervous speaker by drawing on your own experiences of being similarly placed, and by skill perhaps make the audience almost smile aloud, so that he looks up at them and realises he is addressing ordinary and kind human beings. This quality will in fact influence those already mentioned.

The final quality is brevity. To be a competent speaker does not mean that as a chairman you stamp your personality on the proceedings by giving a lengthy speech when you open the meeting or when you close it. This is bad manners, both to the audience and to your guest, the speaker.

What should you do as a chairman before a meeting? As to the speaker, particularly if he is heavily engaged in addressing meetings, confirm how long his speech will last and that he will take questions. Find out if there are any special points he would like you to introduce so as to give him a 'lead-in'. Decide who will repeat questions, whether clumsily put or inaudible. Unless he is highly experienced, do not talk to him in any depth about the subject. Such talking could throw out of poise the final preparation that he has made before arrival. If the meeting is the first of a new branch, of a new society itself or of an 'ad hoc' nature (such as a protest meeting against the building of a new airport), it will be wise to check the administration with the 'honorary secretary'. Make sure the seating, the heating and the ventilation, and the amplifiers (if to be used) are each all right. Is this too elementary? How many have tried to make their way to 'pel' stacking chairs set so close that shins are bumped and tempers accordingly a little frayed? As to ventilation, there was a Commonwealth Prime Ministers' Conference only a few years back where, one afternoon, many present started to nod off. The windows which had been closed at lunch had not been re-opened. 4,000 to 12,000 miles is a long way to come to waste a whole afternoon. Watch the temperature as well *during* the meeting. Returning to consideration of the speaker, be sure he has a reasonable 'lectern', that, from his position, the lighting is all right and that water is provided. Even if you are meeting in a professionally equipped hall, liaison with the management on some of these points is wise.

If you are to have more than four others on the platform with you, a simple diagram showing the seating and orientated to the platform is useful. Suggest that they come on in this order in 'line ahead'. (Do not clutter your platform with unnecessary people. By fidgeting and whispering, they can distract an audience from the speaker.)

It is customary for the speaker to be on the chairman's right. If there is more than one speaker, then they alternate, right and left, of the chair. Start the meeting to time. A good speaker takes latecomers in his stride, and delay, without good reason, is discourteous to those who have taken the trouble to be punctual. If delay seems advisable – if, for example, a coach bringing a large group has broken down but is now underway – take the audience into your confidence and state, with their permission, that you propose awaiting its arrival.

This simple plea turns a disgruntled attitude into a sympathetic one. (Always too take the audience into your confidence if the speaker is held up.)

Your introductory remarks are important. One to three minutes is sufficient; but do not make them so short that the speaker has no time to look around and relax. First, welcome the audience, in one of the countless ways available, remembering that the atmosphere of a meeting begins to be created when the chairman opens his mouth. Stand well and be of good voice.

In introducing the speaker mention only those points which add weight to his authority to speak on his subject. If a speaker is going to talk on an African country, his experience in India and the fact that he once played tennis for England are not necessary. Never read out facts about a speaker; it looks and is discourteous. If, for instance, you were introducing a speaker on Nigeria you might say :

'Sir William Smith was the last Governor of Western Nigeria. But, of course, in the last few years before the country's independence, he was constantly visiting the other two regions. Moreover, Sir William, since retiring, has paid regular yearly visits to Nigeria. Then, as some of you know, he has recently had published a book—*Nigeria's place in the African continent*.'

As to the subject matter (whether you mention this or the speaker first is a matter of choice and circumstance) – introduce this in the most general terms. Do not poach the speaker's likely points. Do not try and commit him to any particular line of approach (a good speaker will laugh this off, but all speakers are not so generous).

Call on the speaker by name ! Do not forget his name and have to search frantically for the paper bearing it. This may sound absurd, until you remember speakers of many nationalities are now addressing meetings. If the name is difficult of pronunciation, is inordinately long, or both, ask the speaker to guide you. He may volunteer a shorter version. If he is an ambassador or a high commissioner, 'His Excellency' will

I

solve the problem. Obedience to this rule is an essential courtesy.

If you are chairing a number of speakers at a conference, then you must be firm in enforcing the time limit allowed to each – in fairness to all of them and to those listening. Otherwise, some of them will have to chop their stride or speak to an audience held back over the allotted time. In both cases, the audience will not be impressed by their chairman. There is no need for rigour. Advise the speakers before you open the session that, if need be, you will pass them a card when, say, three more minutes remain. Bring them to heel gently but firmly if they start to run over the time (a friendly tap of the gavel and a friendly expression – 'I must ask you to wind up, Mr Robinson, in one minute' – and be sure that your order is obeyed). Ensure that the brief message on your card – '3 minutes to go' – is in writing large and legible.

Your duty at a meeting when heckling occurs – nowadays no longer the monopoly of political meetings – has been mentioned at the end of chapter 12, 'Answering Questions'. Your action can be a matter of fine judgement, gauging whether the right to heckle is being abused, how far the personality of the speaker can stand up to it and what is the mood of the audience.

Watch your own bearing when a speaker is in action. Look at him from time to time – with interest! You will wish to make the occasional note. Look also, from time to time, over the audience.

A short break before question time is advisable. It is fair to the speaker, and the audience like to break their silent concentration – to talk quietly and to wriggle. This is fair policy even at lunch hour meetings. Here too is the place to make routine announcements about future meetings, rather than at the end of proceedings, when they sound rather an anticlimax.

The chairman has an important role to play in making question time a useful part of the meeting. Either have a couple of questions to hand yourself, or arrange previously that a member is so armed, in order that you can bridge any gap of shyness when this period begins. Request that members should keep their questions to the point ('. . . so that we may have as many good questions as possible'); that members should stand up ('. . . so that we can see and hear you'); and that their questions should be addressed through the chair ('. . . in case I have to blackball them!'). Such requests want to be made in a friendly racy manner. If the audience shifts in membership at each meeting, it will be wise to give these reminders; but so that they are bearable to the constant members, make sure that you vary the words a little. Warn the audience when there is time for only two more questions – and do not be surprised if you are inundated.

In keeping with the principle of good consolidation in speaking, you want to close a meeting if not with éclat certainly with happy decision. The custom of someone proposing a vote of thanks and another seconding has become rather too formal for most occasions. The courteous alternatives are for you yourself to thank the speaker, or, with a linked sentence of thanks, to call on a member to do so. Beware this does not become an anti-climax; give the proposer some warning, preferably the day before. No artificial perfection is suggested, but if the proposer is at the front or the back, or at the side of the hall where he can traverse widely, this gives the proceedings 'class'.

This vote of thanks should be brief (not abrupt), clearly in a lower tone of authority than the speaker's. Select a point – more than one if appropriate – from the speech and underline it. It is advisable not to break new ground, and certainly not to criticise the speech (or the speaker). For he has no right of reply and, in general, courtesy is a quality to respect. Yet there is no need to ooze platitudinous generalities over his speech; simple thanks can still hide the embarrassment of a poor performance by your guest. It remains for you cheerfully to declare the meeting closed.

16 Television and Radio

Speaking on television is a highly specialised variety of public speaking – so specialised that it has to contradict some of the general principles. It is very necessary to recognise the limitations of this medium, and adapt yourself to them. Strictly, unless televised in a completely natural environment, such as playing games or at work, you cannot appear *quite* natural.

You are speaking only to one or two persons (not to millions). The voice, as in the 'fireside chat' mentioned in chapter 9, must be more conversational in tone, for they are listening in the relaxed intimacy of the living-room. Almost invariably you will be sitting down. Above all, you must remember that you are 'squared off' by the screen. This is fraught with consequences. Part of you only is visible – and, on the one hand, seen at close range; on the other, reduced in size. You are seen through glass; you are seen only in two of the three dimensions. Clearly, therefore, the ability to traverse is strictly limited, if not destroyed; even the expression has to be restrained. A strict self-discipline will be necessary, whilst retaining the essential quality of being natural. Again, in black and white television, your natural colour is drained off and most of your background removed. There is a searchlight glare and accompanying heat. Make-up has to be applied. Appliances and many technicians are all around.

In public speaking proper, members of the audience are seen and heard and their feelings gauged. Speaker and audience are part of one whole, and distinctly felt rhythms of sympathy and antagonism can be built up. There is time to develop and time to absorb a subject. The audience cannot switch off, and will not walk out at once if the start is dull.

The speaker is not minutely observed. He can move and make gestures in a reasonable way. (Even if there is an audience in the studio, the speaker must concentrate either on the lens or the person in the studio to whom he is speaking.)

From this contrast, two further points of importance follow. Unless you are the most experienced of broadcasters, in the estimate of the viewer the visual and, to a slightly less extent, the sound elements of your speech will predominate over the really most important element, the facts and thoughts. Secondly, because of the viewer's ability at once to switch off, and the fact your appearance is usually brief, you must come to the core of your answer, of your argument, *first,* and then give your explanation – being sure to keep it simple. Therefore, with the many differences between speaking in public proper and appearing on television, you cannot do yourself justice without careful preparation. It is the mental preparation that is important rather than the physical.

In passing, it should be stressed that those who offer tuition in public speaking proper by closed circuit television and video-tape recording should examine their sense of responsibility. This equipment is to teach people to speak on television. Undoubtedly, experienced speakers learning to appear on television may indirectly pick up odd points that may improve their normal public speaking. But to baptise newcomers to speaking by this means is quite wrong; there is no short cut to a skill that becomes a way of life.

Stress has been laid earlier on standing well. Sitting well, in this medium, is even more important. For movements that would normally be encouraged as being completely natural in appearance, and that also help you to speak more easily, have to be scaled down. Sit as explained in chapter 6, your 'tail' well back where the seat of the chair meets its back; stomach in, back straight and the body leaning slightly forward from the hips – only slightly, so there is scope to come forward a little more when emphasising important points. Beware of sitting back and relaxing; in the boxed-in close range at which you appear, such posture can give an unfortunate impression of assumed superiority. Likewise keep that back straight; curving the back forward between the shoulder blades gives a shortened and distorted view of the face. Remember, as in standing, the important phrase 'relaxed authority'. You must move in some degree to feel natural; but within such bounds, make it the least possible, for the steady frame of the screen emphasises movement.

As to the hands, even although out of sight, make sure that they are not clasped tightly. Remember that their movements are part of your expression of thought, and therefore tension of the hands can stiffen the features and be disclosed in the eyes. Use them as you would in relaxed quiet conversation. Comfortable and natural as it may be to have the forearms resting along the edge of the table, it is essential to keep them off and have the hands only so placed. Then if the camera for a while shows your body as well, a gesture made at that time will not look like a bunch of bananas being lifted up.

But it is the proper use of the eyes and features that is the key to success. Look always at the person to whom you are speaking. If the viewer, look at the lens; otherwise, at the questioner in the studio. However, be sure that whilst the eyes steadily hold the viewer that they and your features are reflecting your words and that you are moving the head naturally and smoothly – albeit slightly – through various angles. Otherwise your constant look will become a gimlet-like glare which will very soon dismay the viewer. On the other hand, if the expression in the eyes is veiled, you will appear lacking in vitality. From the viewer's angle it is disagreeable to be talked at instead of to.

As stressed in the beginning of this chapter, your expression has to be restrained, yet remain natural. As to looking down, if you are gazing at the lens and do this, the viewer normally thinks that you are unconvincing. He takes it that you are nervous, unfriendly or are furtively reading a note. If notes are necessary, as they may well be for a straight talk, look down at them quite naturally during pauses, and the viewer will understand. If you are speaking to someone in the studio and look down – not an unnatural attitude for thought – the expression of the eyes is hidden and, as said above, you look dull.

Regarding looking up, this is often a nervous habit of speakers, and is apt to disconcert the viewer; you may look to him either pious or mental.

If you are one of a group, invariably the producer will have arranged at the beginning that all of you together will be in view. Yet still be careful how you look sideways or around you. Normally address the person to whom you are replying. If you do sense that you should look as well towards some of the rest, do this steadily. If you begin to imagine that you are in committee and traverse your colleagues too speedily – especially if you dart with your eyes – you risk looking shifty, perhaps in need of help. If you are alone, ignore the technicians in the studio, who can create the illusion that you are in a group.

If in an interview or a discussion, from time to time you wish to reflect shortly before answering, shift the gaze slightly to the side or just above the questioner, so as to allow of concentration of thought. Yet, although you are not looking at the viewer, keep alert in your expression.

Remember how important the expression of the eyes and features is after you have made your important points. In normal responsible conversation you watch another's eyes after saying something to him to be sure that he has understood and to assess his thoughts. It is essential to treat the television viewer just the same. For it is in this pause after speaking, when holding the eye of the listener, that you register goodwill. Your turning away abruptly, or, your eyes losing their expression has an exaggerated effect in this medium. In the first case you may look cross or even frightened; in the second bored or lacking in vitality. The viewer expects you to behave as if you could see him.

In general, a natural smile, here and there, normally blends with the mood of the audience, and puts you at ease.

As to voice and choice of language, keep in mind that you

are speaking only to one or more persons, and, accordingly, retain a friendly but a *crisp* 'fireside manner' – for you must challenge yourself to hold the viewer at all costs. Beware of using the plural, as you might do from time to time in public meetings proper ('all of you . . .', 'my friends . . .' and similar phrases). Brief sentences and simple language remain the rule; but make it disciplined conversational language. Finally, keep in mind that for some reason a pause on television seems twice as long as on radio.

Preparation of what you will say, as always, is of supreme importance. Inherent in television is the fact that many of the matters discussed are topical, even of immediate importance, and therefore the invitation to speak can well be 'within hours'. Complementary to this will be a fairly short allocation of time, say, one to five minutes. Accordingly, when you are to be engaged in discussion or to be interviewed, as said at the beginning you must turn the normal procedure of presentation on its head. Do not in your answer or your contribution start a train of thought which you will have no time to pursue. Do not be tempted to sketch in a background by way of giving proportion to your view or the core of your argument. Introduce such a view or core right away, shortly and clearly – and follow it by simple and lucid explanation (remembering that friendliness in so doing will help). The temptation to follow the usual live 'pattern' and explain first will be great if the questions are 'loaded', but you must keep to this reverse tactic.

As to the preparation for such interview or discussion, remember the invaluable question, 'What is my object?', then ask yourself five others. First, what are the most interesting points I can make? List them, in order of importance, for you will rarely have time to use them all. Secondly, to *whom* are these points interesting? This helps you to phrase the points sympathetically and convincingly. Thirdly, how can I most *briefly* make these points? Fourthly, looking at it from the other side, what 'sticky' questions may I be asked, and can I use any of them to score one of my chosen points? Lastly, what questions would I like to be asked, to fit my chosen points?

You will, outwardly at least, have no notes with you either in an interview or a discussion; but the initial listing of your points and of the possible questions will be invaluable. It will help your speed of selection – the *pace* of television is a new problem for the speaker to notice and conquer. It should also effectively avoid repetition, that can kill interest at once in a short broadcast. Keep relaxed and, within the bounds set by this medium, natural. Keep in mind too that the first sentences – the initial projection – must grip the viewer. Speaking in an interview or a discussion is not a variation of a public speech; it is akin to answering questions after a meeting. (In a discussion – when you have companions – there is much to be said for having brief notes with you. You should have the opportunity to check on a crucial point, such as important statistics, whilst one of your colleagues, your opponents, is speaking. Even if you do not refer to the notes, it is psychologically comforting to know that they are to hand in your pocket.)

In the third type of contribution, a straight talk, notes can be used. Again, you must obey the rule of introducing the core of the argument first and then elucidating it simply. Such a talk, if not recorded, will obviously require a rehearsal by you to check the time. Be sure to speak within your allocation – and so retain Time as your ally to keep you calm and confident.

Nowadays a straight talk may be committed to writing, then projected on a glass screen above or actually across the lens. This is 'cheating' in a high degree – but it need not drain (and must not drain) all the personality out of you, as the foolishness and rudeness of reading a speech in the flesh achieve. Because you are looking the whole time at the lens – and so the viewer – the essential need of looking at the audience is retained. Obviously the speech, to keep the illusion, must be written in the language of speech – short sentences and simple language (flexed with some graphic phrases and some questions); it must be essentially colloquial. Moreover, considerable challenge remains. There is the extra discipline of controlled yet natural movement demanded by the yoke of the screen; the need to use the eyes and the features naturally. An experienced and able speaker may even depart from the text here and there – but only, of course, by way of substitution, not enlargement, for time continues to run. (Unless this departure is of the shortest, on the spur of the moment, you should warn beforehand the technician controlling the timing of the device. Otherwise, seemingly losing his place, he will flap like a prompter in the theatre who has dropped his copy.) This projection of your words may bring you a little closer to the actor; but the method is here and, properly used, gives excellent results. (If the viewer later hears the performer in the flesh, he must not be disappointed if he finds the standard is of a lower calibre.)

What of your notes if you give a straight talk unaided by the projection of a full script on a glass screen? You can do one of two things. Either have an enlargement of the notes mounted on board and then hung below the lens, or, write or type the notes on cards in the normal fashion of a speaker in public. In the latter case, if you look down on them quite naturally, between pauses, the viewer will understand. It is when a speaker pretends he is not consulting notes that the viewer becomes annoyed – either because he realises the pretence, or because the speaker, for a reason he does not understand, looks a little furtive. The less you look down the better. Follow the rule of responsible private conversation and speaking in public of holding the audience's eyes for a moment after making a point, and because you are 'screened off', be sure to lower and raise the head smoothly. (This need to hold the look, to move the head smoothly is a good example of how speaking on television can be a salutary discipline for the able speaker in public, whose most common fault, in his desire to press on with his subject, is the snatching down of the eyes when concluding each thought.) The card or cards will, of course, be tilted – *not* lying flat – either by the support provided or by being held in the palm of the hand. If you adopt the method of having enlarged notes placed under the lens, it is better to glance at them quite naturally, acknowledging you have some form of aid.

Personality is one of the four vital components of a speech. Chapter 5 has analysed the three qualities that reveal the full personality of a speaker – sincerity, friendliness and authority. The concentration on his features imposed by television, together with the limitations it demands, puts the highest premium on a man's natural characteristics. Fortunately the television camera has, as it were, an X-ray quality by which it lays bare artificiality, and thus the three key qualities can only very rarely indeed be assumed or exaggerated. Unfortunately, such qualities can be concealed or even destroyed by a speaker's frame of mind or ignorance of his task – as revealed in chapter 5.

As to dress, television cameras now are not so sensitive to sharp contrasts in tone values. Yet the white stiff collar and the black jacket are still best avoided. For colour television, a woman particularly should dress simply but not drably; colourfully but not garishly. On the positive side, if any adjustment to make-up is needed, the studio experts should be able to cope.

In conclusion, do not be frightened of television. As in speaking to a live audience the main aim is to be and to remain natural. But you have to remember the artificial conditions imposed by this medium cannot but scale down the full movement of body and the expression of features so perfectly natural in normal living conditions. It is a welcome healthy check in these days of mass popularity that television is more likely to show you up than to do you credit. Although it will not disguise mediocrity, although it will not support an illusion of brilliance, it can project so clearly genuine modesty and sincerity. Develop an attitude of mind to your subject which blends equally a sense of humility and a sense of reality. That being said, what upsets the good speaker in public is that far the greater part of the effect on television is likely to come from the 'vision', not the speech itself – from the voice, the eyes, the change of expression and the carriage of the body.

Train yourself to absorb the pace of television – by watching and professionally analysing the good programmes. To end on a down-to-earth note, keep in mind the producer is doing his job regularly and has in mind mainly the public's entertainment. He may not have the time to sense the comparative strangeness of the occasion for you; look after yourself, therefore, pleasantly but firmly.

Sound radio rightly deserves mention. It can often be the better medium for leaving an impression – as so often with music. We talk of speaking but in fact most 'speeches' are being read. Of course your script will simulate conversation. It will have its 'can'ts' and its 'won'ts'; its short sentences and its basically simple language. You may well emulate television in having the core of your argument thrust into the introduction; but in any case see that the introduction is arresting. As in public speaking proper, the conclusion is equally important.

As in a straight talk on television, the length of the speech must be carefully checked. Make time your ally by speaking *within* your allocation – removing any feeling of urgency. For example, in a quarter of an hour's broadcast, use up about fourteen minutes. If you time yourself by the number of written words (a writer's approach), this will be about 1,900 words; but why not have a real rehearsal as described in chapter 2?

Have the script typed on quarto paper; space it well (double or triple spacing – and deeper between paragraphs). It is a good habit not to split sentences between pages, and the bottom of some sheets will therefore remain blank. Use paper that does not rustle and, a subtle tip, back each sheet with blotting paper so that you move it silently over the desk (providing also a pleasant memento for your writing desk for many a month).

Why does speaking give way to reading on sound radio? From the beginning, the BBC found it necessary to see every script beforehand – to prevent the occasional abuse. Again, more relevant to our subject, a loss of words leaves a gap embarrassingly accentuated when the speaker cannot be seen by the audience. More particularly, the strain of speaking when *both* sides are invisible to each other can be great – and most performers are not trained speakers but just specialists in the subject with which they are dealing. As distinct from such straight talk, the preparation for interview and discussion is similar to that for television.

As to delivery, all the good principles of addressing a live audience basically apply; but some of the points television demands have, in a lesser way, been anticipated by radio. Rather akin to the 'fireside chat', modulate your voice as if speaking to one or two people in their living-room. Good pausing is particularly valuable, firstly, between points, so that they may be digested; and secondly, for the sake of good delivery itself. Emphasis, in such a conversational background, is better achieved by speaking more quietly (and more slowly). But you can do this successfully only if you have learnt to throw the voice forward. Remember above all, although you are invisible, to use the hands to emphasise the changes in the voice; and to smile and frown when demanded, which will again appear in your tone.

Just as when using a microphone with a live audience, do not sway to and fro. If you do, the voice will surge like that of the cleric encouraging himself when he feels no response from his congregation. Look away from the script as much as possible – towards the microphone; for, after all, you are supposed to be speaking. A finger or a pencil resting on the script will ensure that you do not lose your place. Do not drop the head lower and lower, but raise the script higher and higher, so that the throat remains flexible and you obey the iron rule of speaking – that your eyes, the notes and the audience are approximately in one line.

17 Conclusion

You cannot learn to play tennis by reading about it. You must go on to the court to practise patiently under expert tuition, and then consolidate your skill by the successes and mistakes of playing in matches. Yet by reading a simple book the intelligent newcomer can gain interest and a 'feel' of the game; whilst the seasoned player can pick up some useful points. The analogy holds for speaking in public. For the inexperienced, reading a book should remove much of the strangeness, often amounting to fear, that surrounds the subject, and should encourage him to meet the challenge. For the speaker of some experience, it should help by strengthening principles of which he is already aware; by bringing to full value those he feels by instinct but has not yet applied; and by revealing some which are entirely new to him.

Then, at least for the newcomer, should come some tuition. It may be that attendance at a good debating society should suffice – bearing in mind the drawbacks and weaknesses of such bodies mentioned in Appendix B, 'The Problem'. Yet they lack the essential sensitive touch of personal criticism that good tuition gives. Membership of such a body is best regarded as a final stage, if need be, to be blended with experience of actual speaking in public. Remember that this subject is unique in its importance as being the way in which those wishing to lead, at all levels of life, mainly express their personalities. Only the artist, in all his variety, expresses himself more strongly through his skill. If personality is to be fully and sincerely *shown*, then the nervous reaction which is almost universal – and which is common to any challenge in life – must be fully understood – and met. It follows that no one can be 'bull-dozed' through this subject, either in quantity

or in haste : either as one of a horde of students, his personality
smothered, or as one of an 'instant' course, cramming a way
of life into a day. Each individual, from every walk of life,
deserves to be treated with firm sensitivity. It is not possible
to stress too much that speaking in public is but the greatest
manifestation of all speaking as it should be. Hence the
subject takes on this heightened value of a way of life, enlarging an individual's capabilities in every respect throughout
the day. It has another merit. It makes you come to grips with
your fears, an experience which must have wider benefits in
the pattern of life.

Constantly remind yourself of the three master keys that
unlock the secret of speaking in public : that, whether you like
it or not, you are disclosing your personality; that nervousness
is natural, and is an asset to be harnessed; that *any* speech is
but an enlargement of a responsible conversation with another.

Tuition in Britain tends to be available either at courses
run for businessmen by numerous bodies or by individuals;
or at schools of dramatic art. The former are inclined to be
too practical, missing the finer points; the latter are naturally
prone to stress the element of speech training. This is a pity,
for it is the *whole* man who wants to be trained to discover
himself.

How long is required to provide anyone – from the chairman
of a leading company, through all the professions to the trade
union official and the foreman; from a man in his twenties to
a man in his sixties – with the necessary foundations? Given
high quality tuition on the one side and clear thinking co-
operation on the other – with no suggestion of cramming – five
sessions of around two and a half hours each suffice. One
session weekly is the ideal, so that the 'pupil' can live with
his short speeches in odd moments and prepare them carefully.
A set of good notes, recording all a tutor has said in his
complementary talks, are the pupils' right. A group of four
is the ideal number; six is the absolute maximum.

As with any technique, in art, in work or in games, the

speaker must seek out every reasonable opportunity to retain and improve his skill. He is fortunate in that the subject is so much more than speaking on the feet. Provided he remains natural, he can almost throughout the day pick up experience. Also, apart from his own efforts, he can learn from the faults and merits that he now studies critically of other public speakers. He may get more enjoyment from good theatre, watching the way the best actors carry themselves and speak. He may find, after a while that literally three or four sessions of voice training may consolidate the principles and the demonstration of voice production that the main course must provide. Such training, although it can be individual, is most effective and most interesting in groups of three. Not only does it increase confidence – and so authority – but makes speaking so much easier.

The tape recorder deserves particular mention as an invaluable aid to a tutor, especially when he is coaching an individual for a specific speech. It endorses beyond contradiction his advice to shed the puppy fat and leave just the sinew and bone of clear language and lucid fact and thought. It allows him to show how a speech can be transformed by proper pausing and the change of pace; how the dropping of the voice can be avoided; how the expression of the eyes and on the features can alter the voice. The speaker, having heard the vast change he himself has made in his speech, goes away full of happy confidence.

As stated in the Preface, this book is for all – for man and for woman from every walk of life, for the young and the mature; but at this time in history it is directed particularly at the senior members of management and the members of key professions. They must realise that it is their right and duty to be as proficient in expressing themselves lucidly aloud as in their daily administrative and executive skills. It is quite extraordinary how leaders of industry and commerce so often take it for granted that there should be a yawning gap between their expertise in business and their expertise in speech. The two should not so much be complementary as interwoven. It is humiliating not only for the speaker but also for his audience to see and hear a man of standing acting so often in such a low key of intelligence. Speaking is a deed, and a deed of great value and, often, of consummate skill. As such it is the rightful possession not only of the thinker proper but also of the man of action.

Remember that speaking in public really amounts to a display of good manners. Mastering the techniques, as with all skills, entails some artificiality, and every new habit in formation is tedious. But if you discipline yourself with rules, then one day you become free of them all. The eventual aim is to be quite natural.

Here, in mastery of this subject, is surely a joker in the pack for industry and commerce, of increasing importance as the export side of trade has to grow. Here is a weapon, almost ready-made and unique to us – quality speaking of the economic and scientific language of the world – *our* language.

K

Appendices

Appendix A

EXAMPLES OF 'NOTES'

1. THAT FOR WESTERN MAN LIFE HAS LOST ITS CHALLENGE (INTRODUCTION ONLY)
2. JUVENILE DELINQUENCY
3. STUDENT UNREST
4. AN ADDRESS AT A NATIONAL BUSINESS CONFERENCE (PART ONLY)
5. AN AFTER-LUNCHEON BUSINESS ADDRESS (INTRODUCTION ONLY)
6. A TOAST BY A CHAIRMAN AT HIS COMPANY'S STAFF DINNER AND DANCE
7. A TOAST AT A DINNER TO A RETIRING COLLEAGUE
8. A PRESIDENT'S SPEECH AT A YACHT CLUB'S ANNUAL DINNER

Chapter 3 stresses that notes are very much a personal affair. They are the speaker's own shorthand. Accordingly, some of the examples which are given may be in parts difficult to follow. Yet the *layout*, in its variety, remains of interest for all to consider. This may vary according to your knowledge of the subject; according to the subject itself – whether it is a simple or a detailed one; according to how deep you are probing into the subject in relation to the type of audience that you are addressing. From another angle, bear in mind that the lighting at an evening function, particularly a dinner, may be poor or dim – your spacing and words must be enlarged. Always be sure, in words and layout, to keep the notes *simple*. The challenge of finding the words and phrases, of using your voice to help their meaning, must not be dulled by too elaborate a note.

It was thought an advantage for the first example to add a version of the speech based on the notes.

1.   THAT FOR WESTERN MAN
                    LIFE HAS LOST ITS CHALLENGE

'Mr President, Sir, ... there is an old Chinese proverb that
runs something like this : "If people spoke *only* on subjects on
which they were *qualified* to speak, then the World would be
filled with *profound* and *dignified* . . . . *silence* !"

'My feeling tonight is, however, that this is a subject of
such general interest that we can all "have a go".

'The motion before the House sits particularly on the shoulders of youth – with the world before him, before her. I speak
as a young man, thankful to have the privilege of being in this
stage of development. Moveover, I am engaged in the most
natural of occupations, where we all know what the challenge
of Nature herself means – farming. Nevertheless I feel – and
see it reflected in the attitude of so many today – that Life
has, for the time, in large part lost much of its challenge.
I say, "for the time", because challenge of some sort is in the
end vital for man's existence.

'Just after the last War, one of the greatest of men, General
Smuts, said : "The World has struck its tents and again is on
the march". Little did he realise how widely his remark was
to apply as the years sped on.

'The problem is a paradoxical one. On the one hand, on
the home front, there is too much security – and entertainment – for too many, so as to blunt their senses to life's
battle, so as to take away the positive side of fear. On the
other hand, on the world front, so complicated is life becoming that the thinking man at least is numbed, bewildered,
feels he is unled. The cold war has not yet ended; the new
developing countries have painfully and patiently to find their
feet; science introduces invention after invention – for govern-
ments' and industry's use; economic rivalry between the na-
tions intensifies – whilst the great problems of race relations,
population increase, food production and control of nuclear
power stand behind all.

'I propose developing my case first by looking . . . . . .'

(This requires about 2½ minutes to *speak*; about a tenth of a 25 minutes speech.)

FOR WESTERN MAN LIFE LOST CHALLENGE

I. INTRODUCTION

    A. Chinese Proverb . . . but tonight . . .

    B. Youths' shoulders – privilege – challenge of Nature –
       a farmer YET . . .

    C. Smuts

    D. Paradoxical Problem—

        Home Front – too much {Security / Entertaint.

                    Senses blunted
        World –   highly complicated
                    Man {numbed / feels unled
                    'cold war'
                    developing countries
                    Science
                    Economic rivalry
                    race relations
                    population increase
                    food production
                    control Nr power

(Write the quotations out on the back of the card. Read them through calmly just before the President announces the debate, taking in carefully their sense. The notes of all speakers after the first should leave a wider margin – for marking up, by sign or word, where an added comment should be made to neutralise more strongly what an opponent has said.)

2.   JUVENILE DELINQUENCY

1. *Introduction*	present Crime Wave How much is 'J.D.'? 'Spare the Rod . . .'
2. *What is?*	several Opinions not just Dress Ton-up Boys Cycle chains, Knives Gangs
3. *What Causes?*	TV unhappy Home Working Mothers School – Discipline? no Corporal Punishment no Leadership Coffee Bars Drugs
4. *What Punishment is Received?*	Fines/Probation Detention Centres Remand Homes Approved Schools Borstal/Prison
5. *What Other Punishment?*	Corporal Punishment Stocks?
6. *Conclusion*	Borstal Allocation centres (2) Keep Psht and Cure distinct

(Sufficient material for a 10 minute or 40 minute talk.)

3.   STUDENT UNREST

A. INTRODUCTION   1/

  1. *Different Student of Today –*
      vast increase in Numbers (c 200,000)
      different Background
      Grants universal
      vast Range $\begin{cases} \text{of Colleges} \\ \text{of Subjects} - \end{cases}$
                                    vocational
                                    general education
      Facilities often bad in $\begin{cases} \text{Size} \\ \text{Quality} \end{cases}$
                                    (because of hasty forming)

  2. Universities – now 40+

      Before 1600   6 $\begin{cases} 2 \text{ England} \\ 4 \text{ Scotland} \end{cases}$

      19th Cy   5 $\begin{cases} 4 \text{ England} \\ 1 \text{ Wales} \end{cases}$

      1900 – 1938   8 $\begin{cases} 7 \text{ England} \\ 1 \text{ N. Ireland} \end{cases}$

      1950s   4

      1960s   20 $\begin{cases} 16 \text{ England} \\ 4 \text{ Scotland} \end{cases}$

      (Univy status to colls of techy.)

2/

B. CAUSES OF UNREST

   1. *USA*

      huge campuses – impersonal
      shock of Vietnam
      shock of Race Relations
      . . . . . .
      . . . . . .

   2. *France*

      Unlimited students
      So lack {of facilities / of teachers
      strictness of regime
      . . . . . .
      . . . . . .

   3. *W. Germany*

      Old-fashioned {Rigidity of
      Autocratic {Professors
      . . . . . .
      . . . . . .

3/

4. *Yugoslavia*

. . . . . .
. . . . . .
. . . . . .

5. *Britain*

'Success' of LS of Economics' sit-in over new Director
(Rhodesia)
vast increase in numbers
facilities often lacking
many of 'teachers' accelerated (irresponsible)

. . . . . .

C. OUTSIDE INFLUENCES/COMMON GROUND?

1. Aggravated by TV and Press (everywhere)
2. Aggravated by Police (*save*, Britain)
3. Some Communist influence (fan the flames)

. . . . . .
. . . . . .

(D. IMMEDIATE EFFECTS

E. FUTURE EFFECTS . . . would follow, each with the five
sub-headings of heading B.)

4.   AN ADDRESS AT A NATIONAL BUSINESS
CONFERENCE
(Part only)

1/

IMPROVING OVERSEAS OPERATIONS
I. INTRODUCTION

A Coy MUST {to Consolidate Perfce
Grow . . .   {to lay Foundns. Future
Opportunities in many Guises

THE Coy = who {recognises them
                         {exploits them

2 Principal Ways – {deeper Penetration Markets
                          {Diversification

II. MARKET PENETRATION

A. Performance Coy – THE Yardstick, return on Capital
employed: BUT others vital too –
Market Share (closely gdd secret!)
What Organisation, Distributive Pattern?
Varies –
different Products – d Treatment
different Markets – d Patterns

2/

B. YET SOME GUIDELINES:

Mistake to be too Self-Sufficient

Encourage growth Independently owned Associates (to distribute products)

In Emerging Countries, great value of encouraging local Self-Reliance

Form of such 'Independents'? –
established Entrepreneurs
locally owned Distributors
even Newcomers – { no knowledge
{ no funds!

Give 'It' its head – BUT hold the Reins! (the Initiative)

C. KNOW YOUR MARKET – for Old and New Product

Market Survey essential –
principles scientifically assessed –
distribution pattern established
sales programme established
manufacture geared

3/

YET,

1. Must have *some* sales orgn of own
(from travelling rep with rented desk to a full organisation)

Coy Sales Force to have
⎰deep knowledge product
⎱good sales technique

2. Must *Stimulate* demand –

a. Advertising ⎰National
⎱Regional

b. Public Relations

DON'T deny being 'Foreign'
⎰recognise local hopes
⎱glamour of Industrialisatn

Harness release of Creative Endeavour loosened by
Political Independence

3. Then Tie 'Independent' closely to self by maximum
support.

a. *Indirectly* –
PR
Advertising
Market Research
Product Development

4/

b. *Directly*—

advice {customer service
       {equipment

training} sales, technical
staff   }

specialist   (systems
assistance − {records
              {warehousing
              {stock
              (financial} control

If Product Technical −
    regular Advisory Service for Users

Assistance in Sales Promotion
                    (point of sale
                    {direct mailing
                    {s/promotion weeks
                    (dealer conferences

        later, Bonuses, Credit Terms

D. IN SUM −

make Product consumer wants
promote Brand Image
Distributor has worthwhile living
THEN, by all aids, make him Depdt on you.

(III. DIVERSIFICATION
  A. HORIZONTALLY
  B. VERTICALLY
  C. BY ACQUISITION
IV. CONCLUSION . . . . would follow.)

5.   AN AFTER-LUNCHEON BUSINESS ADDRESS
(Introduction only)

I. INTRODUCTION

Pleasure in reviewing our prospects

Our commanding new HQ in Britain

Address of 7 Heads:

Some Simple *Trade Figures*

Increased *Population* – Significance

Problems to Face

Imptce. Good *Deliveries*

Imptce. Good *Promotion*

Our Countrymen in GB

The Mechanics of Export

(Narrow card to be in the palm of the hand and to be raised up and forward for reference – or, to be cupped in the rim of a port or brandy glass.)

6. A TOAST BY A CHAIRMAN AT A COMPANY'S STAFF DINNER AND DANCE

I. WELCOME

II. SOCIAL CLUB
Its happy strength
Praise – staff, committee
Events of Year –
......
......
......

III. FOOTBALL CLUB
Review/ 3 Highlights {league / cup / tour abroad}

Praise of Captain
Leg-pull {Dusty Miller / Streaky Brown}

IV. CRICKET CLUB
As member MCC, critical!
three teams now
praise Groundsman (Harry Smith)
saw Div'l Final:
batting of Roy Clark
bowling of Don Jones
our Milburn in size! –
Ian Todd.

V. OUR BUSINESS
Diff't Natl Background
Our Team Spirit

VI. TOAST

(Half-cards, to nestle in the palm of the hand and to be raised up and forward for reference – or, to be cupped in the rim of a port or brandy glass. Heading V should be light-hearted but responsible in tone; shrewd and reflective, if need be; never heavy or long.)

A TOAST AT DINNER TO A RETIRING COLLEAGUE

7.

1/

I. Happy but Reflective occasion – for John particularly

Nearly 40 yrs with us (vast changes World)

Balliol, Ox, 1925-8

i First met M/car! – bull-nosed Morris

ii mark Bl Tradition –

Macmillan   Healey

Kilmuir   Roy Jenkins

Heath

Harold Nicolson

Toynbee

Joined Coy 1929

unusual then Graduate in industry

2/

II. S. AFRICA – 10 yrs

District Manager, B

Contemporaries present tonight! –

John Marshall

Dick Harris

Jock Mackay

influence on Golf

Fishing story!

III. AUSTRALIA – 7 yrs

M. Director

Contemporaries present –

Bill Green

Johnny Stout

up-country riding incident!

L

3/

•

IV. HQ LONDON

Experience to use new Managerial
Structure

Decentralisation

Shrewd Selector Staff

Rapid Addn Overseas Invst

Story of my Visit with him to Argentine!

V. JOHN'S INTERESTS
(Mary, Wife's support)

VI. FUTURE?
NEDDY – Yachting – charity work

VII. PRESENTATION: TOAST

(Half-cards, to nestle in the palm of the hand and to be raised up and forward for reference – or, to be cupped in the rim of a port or brandy glass.)

8. THE COMMODORE'S SPEECH AT A YACHT CLUB'S ANNUAL DINNER

I. WELCOME
   Members & Guests
   Sir George Saltwater
   Commodore Lars Luthman
   M. René Duplay

II. ANNUAL REVIEW
   Membership (& Sub) Increase (1829 to 2002)
   new Pontoon
   Changing Rooms/ Hot Water
   Club Boatman
   Flower Arrgts. (Mrs D)
   Notable Cruises {PL to Iceland {RK to Patagonia
   Tribute to Secretary

III. 'ROUND-THE-WORLD SINGLE-HANDED'
   A. *Chichester/Rose*
      Courage Unique in all history
      24 hr Loneliness/Faith Age!
      Cf. Them: their Boats
   B. Current Race
      Merits and cautions
      practicability
      involvement Rescue Services
      lessons we may learn
      '*All* round-the-world sailors at heart'

IV. TOAST

(Half-cards, to nestle in the palm of the hand and to be raised up and forward for reference – or, to be cupped in the rim of a port or brandy glass.)

L*

Appendix B

THE PROBLEM

In the broad sweep, industry and commerce and all the professions have at the moment no realistic conception of effective speaking – more particularly, of speaking in public. The view is essentially a negative one, of the need just to fill some vague fictitious gap in the past of countless employees and members. Yet in industry and commerce 'communications', fundamental to the fighting services in a scientific sense since the First World War, is now a word often spoken with such hushed reverence that it does seem extraordinary that the human voice – the core of all communication – is not given more attention. So little attention of the right sort is needed for such great results.

In large organisations the subject, if taught at all, is invariably the preserve of that conscientious person, the education or training officer. He, not unnaturally, puts it into the general programme of training – to become just another scalp on the manager's or junior executive's 'course' belt. Again, bearing in mind his budget, he is apt to accept a tender for tuition that puts the quality of a course in jeopardy. Then, finding the instruction so mediocre, he may try taking the subject himself, or delegating it to one of his staff. Accordingly it almost invariably receives scant treatment. Yet mastery of it is a skill that underpins nearly all that a good executive has to do; the subject is too fundamental to be just one of education. To shell men out like peas on too crowded a course in too short a time; not to spread tuition sufficiently to allow each to prepare with patience short yet responsible speeches; not to give them permanent written notes of the principles lectured on – is worse than useless. A man's last state may become worse than his first, his nervousness or fear in no way mollified, whilst the subject remains in his eyes ridiculous or hated. The key point, that each man's individuality is involved in such tuition, is ignored.

What is the attitude of the many schools, colleges and institutes running managerial courses, whether sponsored or inspired by the government or run by able management consultants? Hundreds of organisations each spend thousands of pounds every year sending staff on external courses. Few, if any, of such courses offer real tuition in effective speaking, although most pay lip service to its need. One national college realistically advises students not so equipped before arrival to become so. Some let a member of the staff, specialising in another subject, 'amateur' his way through giving instruction. Others ease their conscience by seeking inspiration in one visiting lecture. Surely for an organisation to send, at considerable expense, a chosen executive on a high quality course – where case studies and discussions involving group leadership abound – when he is ill-equipped in the technique of speaking, is like entering a pedigree dog at Cruft's international dog show with cataract of the eyes. A thread of able instruction in this subject woven into the first three or four weeks of a general course would give colour and strength in its own right, and would also mutually give to and gain from the rest of the course's pattern more colour and strength.

Meanwhile, those who until further notice most urgently require this skill, the members of the board and senior management, remain outside the training officer's brief and are rarely able to will themselves as individuals to make the time to seek out tuition. More and more as industry and commerce increase their power outwardly, and inwardly enrich themselves by employing as salaried staff so many of the professions, and by taking over the brains that once would have gone to the administration of an empire, must the chairman, the managing director and their colleagues learn, if not to stride with the Queen's Counsel, at least to be competent speakers. This ability is a right that belongs to any man with a semblance of leadership. It is a question of discovering himself – pulling out the latent part of his nature which, for various reasons, he has allowed to sleep. Countless chairmen and managing directors worry themselves almost to illness when a public speech looms ahead. Many, with a conscience, as they sidestep speech after speech, acquire permanently a measure of inferiority complex. 'Image' has now so often a tarnished meaning, but there is no doubt that any large organisation gains immeasurably in the jockeying of national and international life if it has a natural and sincere spokesman at its head. A good speech also, at the right time, might be worth six months' skilled administrative effort.

The professions, in their more individual way, are equally in the stocks. If any subject has to be dropped in a training college for the clergy who are digesting too heavy a syllabus, it is likely to be instruction in speaking. The Bar since the last Great War can well take notice that skill in speaking comes not as a gift from Heaven. Dons, at least at Oxford and Cambridge, remain in most cases as bad as ever. The fact that their major interest may be research is no excuse for failing to give lucid instruction to the thousands of students needing guidance, perhaps inspiration. (With the vast expansion in university education that is now planned, it surely is a duty to see that when they lecture those of such outstanding intellect are able to express themselves clearly.) The accountant and the solicitor, probing their way more and more into the administrative side of the business world, need mastery of this quality. As important as any are the scientist and the technologist. Today is very much their world, a creation of enormous responsibility for their thinking minds. If the call of duty makes them surrender some of their professional independence and take up a fair share of key administrative posts, in government service and in industry, then particularly they owe to themselves and to those they lead to be lucid in spoken thought.

When should this subject be taught? This is a decision deserving very careful thought. Save for the 'fliers' and the professions based on speaking – the Bar, the Church and the University – 25 to 35 years of age is a comfortable bracket. Somewhere within this span a man has shed his puppy fat, and academic and professional qualifications are out of the way. The essential feature is that a few years' experience of practical life gives the necessary cutting edge to his appreciation of proper use of the subject. To be sure, those older, certainly up to 65, can be successfully taught. Indeed, the full value of effective natural speaking may be more apparent, with his wider horizon, to the man in his forties or fifties (but then there are so many unnecessary wasted years to bewail). Certainly there is an enormous leeway to be made up in this country among the maturer generations.

What about debating societies? Debating societies at school and university have their merits – but they have their dangers too. They can give a boy or a student a measure of confidence in hearing his voice in a different key from that of conversation; in being on his feet; in being in pleasant dispute. But unless gently warned by a wise master or mature friend respectively, he can believe it to be an ultimate achievement to stand up for five minutes and talk cleverly on nothing. Such 'gift of the gab' is anathema to the practical leaders in life. Occasions do occur in public and business life when saying little in facts, within the bounds of integrity, is essential; but the real speaker, with his overall mastery, takes this exception in his careful stride.

Again, study alone does not give the required maturity. The sinews of fact and thought are almost invariably subordinated to the cleverness of language, thus reversing the fundamental balance of responsible speaking. Further, the machinery of debate – points of explanation and of order, quibbles on the minutes – is apt to be playfully employed by the ardent debater and to loom too large in its fussiness.

The maturer nature and the freedom of the university debating societies can, of course, be of great value to the future barrister, who will ultimately be disciplined by his appearance in court. One would like to say the same about the potential politician. But he has no judge later to cut him down to size; nor is humility, which will permit self-criticism, a prominent characteristic of his. So many leading lights at university debating societies are 'little-old-men-cut-shorter', who never seem to enjoy any natural youth.

Should the subject be taught more professionally at school or at university? As is suggested above, this allows of no measured experience of life, to balance the pupil's learning; it would make the average student precocious. Certainly attention could be given just to training the voice – if presented in an interesting way. Elocution, through the artificial way it was once conducted, has left a cloud of suspicion over such training, although the girls' schools seem so much more sensible than the boys' in realising the value of good natural speaking.

The conclusion must be that it is each profession, that it is industry and commerce themselves and the many bodies which run or advise on courses – colleges and institutes, management consultants' study centres, national industry training boards – which should be responsible for such instruction.

It is fair to say that industry and commerce (and the professions) have many good excuses for not looking this subject straight in the eyes. A mystique has at times been deliberately built around it, playing on the nervousness so often encountered. Again, priding himself on his standing as a man of action, the top executive gains encouragement to shrink within himself by his contempt for the impersonal patter of not a few salesmen and the factless loquacity of not a few politicians. Further, he sees national figures in business showing great discourtesy to their audience by reading their speeches (a contradiction in terms if ever there was one). Then, as mentioned in chapter 3, national bodies raising a conference aggravate the matter by talking and writing of speakers 'reading papers', and demanding copies of speakers' scripts weeks, if not months, ahead; and the Press, often encouraged by the habits of those convening conferences, have come to expect a handout as of right on every occasion. Feeling himself an amateur as a speaker, the senior executive is apt to bow to the routine of administration and the routine of prestige demanded by the organisers – and to use a copy of his long-flowing written script. Thus the major object of the conference – to put over facts and thoughts in as stimulating a way as possible – is defeated.

Industry and Commerce have every inducement to raise their sights considerably in mastering the subject of public speaking – not only in its own right but also as a happy discipline throughout the day. The initial move must essentially come from the boardroom.

Appendix C

CHURCHILL

Winston Chuchill is said to have read his speeches on most occasions. Lloyd George is said, in the main, to have memorised his. Such statements, without explanation, appear to undermine all the principles set out in a book such as this. When the facts are examined, they are bound to support them. It would be more accurate to say that, given the occasion and time allowing, Churchill *acted* his speeches. He knew how vital it was to look at his audience almost continuously – which reading never allows – and to change his expression, gesture naturally and have some movement of the body so as to affect the vigour or reflection of his speech. He had much of his text imprinted on his mind by 'living with it', by working over it by dictation and re-dictation, and by discussing with others both its ideas and presentation.

From the beginning of his public life he was speaking against a background of great moment. This feeling was intensified beyond parallel in the Second World War, when he spoke with the greatest public issues at stake, and every word had to be counted; when through broadcasting his audience were countless millions throughout the world whose morale could be greatly uplifted by what he said. He was conscious too of the fact that many of his speeches, or major passages from them, would be read by millions more than had heard them spoken.

Such speeches were usually set out on high quality very thick paper, the size of cards, and nearly as rigid. There was no question of the script being longflowing, like a *Times'* leader or the page of a book. To the casual eye it consisted of notes, set out rather like couplets of verse or a psalter, with ample spaces between. But closer observation revealed these 'couplets' were in fact separate sentences or separate thoughts, yet, in the tradition of notes, with many of their words abbreviated.

To understand how Churchill came to favour this detailed method of preparation, almost from the beginning, requires some knowledge of his early life and of the background of his times. For so varied and considerable was his experience in speaking in public before he entered Parliament, that such meticulous attention seemed quite unnecessary.

He had been rather a rebel at Harrow, and it was only soon after he was commissioned, in his first few months in India with his regiment, that he started his intense self-education. He had Lady Randolph, his mother, send out to him countless selected volumes for reading, and during the long midday halt to regimental duties he read voraciously four to five hours daily. To achieve this intensity of reading he blended his studies, at the one extreme reading Gibbon's *Decline and Fall of the Roman Empire* and Macaulay's lyrics and history; at the other, Plato's *Republic,* Aristotle's *Politics* and other works of philosophy. Equally important to the knowledge acquired and the thought engendered was the appreciation born for graphic language. Those who know their Gibbon, especially if from time to time, they read aloud the odd phrase, can see how his style imperceptibly affected the style of Churchill in speech.

The inspiration of this reading gave him an insight into his political ability and strengthened his resolution that public life was the only career for him. The feeling of destiny, that was soon to grip him so strongly, was encouraged. Whilst on leave at home, he accordingly sought, through the Conservative Office, opportunities to speak, and two years later, in 1899, encouraged by success, he resigned his commission. Within three months, he fought a by-election at Oldham, and although he lost, he had the experience of speaking at least three to four times daily to the packed keen audiences of the time – making speeches 'involuntarily' as he wrote at the time to a friend.

His Boer War adventure over, he contested Oldham again at the general election in September 1900. In those days, general elections were not affairs of one day but were spread over three to six weeks, and his success at Oldham was one of the first results announced. In consequence, he was made for three packed weeks to address meetings in key marginal seats throughout the country, supporting the great leaders of his party, Salisbury, Balfour and Chamberlain – meetings of 5,000 to 6,000 men electors.

Then he put off taking his seat in Parliament until February, and undertook a tour of five weeks lecturing nightly about his experience in the Boer War. Leading figures of the land chaired most of these meetings. A similar tour of twelve weeks immediately followed in the United States and Canada.

Four days after entering the House of Commons, now 26 years of age, Churchill made his maiden speech. He followed young Lloyd George on a motion about the war. Yet, against the concentrated and varied experience he had already had of speaking in public, it is interesting to read what he wrote of this event in his book, *My Early Life,* written in 1930.

> In those days, and indeed for many years, I was unable to say anything (except a sentence in rejoinder) that I had not written out and committed to memory beforehand . . . (page 380)

– and he goes on to regret lacking the varied experience in speaking enjoyed by those at a university. For one so strongly believing in his destiny and so recently and deeply blooded in speaking on public events, often in the company of the most eminent public men of the day, this seems an extraordinarily modest approach. But these were still the days when many great orators sat in Parliament and speeches were given a prominence undreamed of in our modern times. Moreover, as the son of one of the greatest men of the previous generation, who had died tragically in his forties, Winston

Churchill was the centre for all eyes. The speech was a success, and it is of interest to note that the *Daily Telegraph* reported that he held a modest page of notes in his hand but rarely had to refer to it, and mentioned also his lively gestures.

It seems probable too that from the beginning Churchill wished to ensure that the quality of his language matched the quality of his thoughts – in his later serious writings as well as in his great speeches he was painstaking in his selection of the right word or phrase. This being so, the tendency not only to have full notes but also to memorise would surely be strengthened through the impediment from which he suffered. He would want to rehearse his speeches aloud to ensure he did not muff the key words and phrases. Mr Randolph Churchill, in the memoirs he began to write, said this impediment could have been a stammer or a lisp – like his father Winston Churchill had difficulties over pronouncing the letter 'S'. Early in his life he was assured by a specialist there was no organic defect. In his first year in Parliament, his frequent speaking and lecturing began to cure him of this handicap and so helped him to lose the inhibition which, from time to time, it had naturally caused him. Mr Randolph Churchill went on to say –

Those who heard him talk in middle and old age may conclude that he mastered the inhibition better than he did the impediment. Indeed, he may have unconsciously exploited the residual impediment to advantage in order to achieve a wholly individual style of public oratory. (Vol. II, pages 29-30.)

Moreover, akin to Wavell's ability to remember poetry, Churchill had the gift of memorising what he chose to and, early in life, had memorised many of his father's speeches.

Two final reflections remain concerning his style of speaking. First, apart from the influence of Gibbon on his choice of language, it was an American politician of Irish descent, never to achieve lasting prominence in public life, who influenced his oratorical delivery. Mr Randolph Churchill describes how when Churchill gained permission, whilst still garrisoned in Britain, to observe the insurrection in Cuba, he stayed on his way in New York with Bourke Cockran, a lawyer and a member of Congress. Churchill was 21 and his host 41. Although he never heard him speak in public, Churchill was deeply and permanently impressed by the outstanding quality of Cockran's conversation, and corresponded with him for some years. Just over fifty years later, in his great speech at Fulton, he mentioned the influence of Bourke Cockran; and Adlai Stevenson, a few years after this, recalled that Churchill confided in him how 'An American statesman taught me how to use every note of the voice like an organ'.

Secondly, the danger of memorising speeches is well illustrated in Volume II of the Memoirs. In 1904, speaking in a debate on the Trades Union and Trade Disputes Bill, Churchill broke down because he had lost the thread of his argument after three-quarters of an hour, and sat down mumbling apologies.

> Until then Churchill's speeches had indeed been most thoroughly prepared; but he tried to deliver many of them in the House of Commons by learning them by heart beforehand. Churchill hardly ever again ventured to make a public speech without the fullest, almost verbatim, notes to guide him. (page 79)

Lloyd George, as mentioned above, was said to have memorised his speeches in the main. But he also was a genius. It is not difficult to imagine one of his poetic flair in those days of oratory when the hustings were not challenged by radio or television, and when his speeches were of the generalities of politics in which he was daily living, knowing his facts almost by heart. It would be largely a matter of choosing and chiselling them to fit the occasion.

Memorising can mean two different things. You can memorise a speech like lines of poetry where every word counts, or you can just memorise the sequence of your facts and thoughts. The former is the dangerous practice. The latter applies to a skilled and relaxed speaker performing without notes, who would be able to retain all the freedom of expression and bodily movement that must be part of good speaking. (Indeed a speaker *with notes* should have the main framework of his speech in mind – hence why giving the subject thought well before the speech, living gently with it, is so important.) What has been said about Churchill shows that there is no comparison between 'reading' a speech as he so often did and reading a speech as practised by so many people today. Apart from the fact that his speeches were made, from his entry into public life, at the highest national level, or, outside the House dealt with the highest national issues, the layout of his script, although in complete sentences, resembled most closely notes proper. Nowadays, those who at all levels of meetings read their speeches do so from flowing scripts, as full as an article in a journal; do so in a reader's tone; and do so hardly looking at their audience. They, in all their variety, read out of weakness, occasionally blended with laziness.

Moreover, at least in the last two decades of his active life – from becoming Premier – Churchill rarely in the preparation of his speeches himself wrote out any parts of them. He would summon one of his secretaries, as inspiration came to him, to take down his thoughts – wherever he might be, at whatever time. From the resultant clippings and from discussions of the subject with others, a final dictation would result, like or akin to that so happily described by Sir Robert Menzies in his Syme memorial lecture in Melbourne in 1963 – and now in his book, *Afternoon Light*. Churchill, pacing up and down, would test every phrase, for its meaning, for its weight and for its effect in sound. His final choice was indicated to his secretary by the authority that entered his tone.

Acting a speech as Churchill did from a full script or from memory is a further dimension of speaking, which those of high skill, blooded in prepared and impromptu speaking, can undertake on notable occasions. Barristers, given the need, will do so in their final address to the court. Birkenhead, Churchill's great friend, with all his unrivalled fluency and agility of brain, wrote and memorised his first speech before a London judge and jury – at the Old Bailey – taking advantage of the fact it was a plea in mitigation which accordingly could be prepared fully in advance. A novice speaker, no matter how outstanding in his profession or business, attempting to emulate such a method must fail. He would be drained of all spontaneity; of all authority, sincerity and friendliness – the key characteristics of good speaking; and personality, a vital component of a speech, would vanish.

It remains to say that this luxury for the experienced speaker of acting a speech of moment requires no little time for preparation; preparation, too, spread over quite a period so that the subject becomes part of him, sinks deeply into his mind. No public figure, especially when in office, could make this an invariable habit. If he could, he would, of course, defeat his purpose. For the experience of free natural speaking, from which this ultimate method springs, would wither and, without such root this acting, by detailed notes or memorising word by word, would reveal its inherent artificiality.

Index

Bold type indicates main entries, which precede other entries